A GUIDE TO ORAL HISTORY
AND THE LAW

| | |

A GUIDE TO ORAL HISTORY
AND THE LAW

| | |

JOHN A. NEUENSCHWANDER

OXFORD
UNIVERSITY PRESS
2009

OXFORD
UNIVERSITY PRESS

Oxford University Press, Inc., publishes works that further
Oxford University's objective of excellence
in research, scholarship, and education.

Oxford   New York
Auckland   Cape Town   Dar es Salaam   Hong Kong   Karachi
Kuala Lumpur   Madrid   Melbourne   Mexico City   Nairobi
New Delhi   Shanghai   Taipei   Toronto

With offices in
Argentina   Austria   Brazil   Chile   Czech Republic   France   Greece
Guatemala   Hungary   Italy   Japan   Poland   Portugal   Singapore
South Korea   Switzerland   Thailand   Turkey   Ukraine   Vietnam

Published by Oxford University Press, Inc.
198 Madison Avenue, New York, New York 10016

www.oup.com

Oxford is a registered trademark of Oxford University Press.

Library of Congress Cataloging-in-Publication Data
Neuenschwander, John A.
A guide to oral history and the law / John A. Neuenschwander.
p.   cm.
Includes index.
Summary: "The new edition covers legal release agreements; defamation; copyright; the Internet;
Institutional Review Boards (IRBs), oral history as evidence; the duty to report a crime;
teaching considerations. It includes examples of best practices and legal precautions. The areas
that receive particular attention are legal release agreements, safeguards for protecting
interviews online; and procedures to protect against defamation"—Provided by publisher.
ISBN 978-0-19-536597-9; 978-0-19-536596-2 (pbk.)
1. Privacy, Right of—United States.   2. Copyright—United States.   3. Contracts—United States.
4. Historians—Legal status, laws, etc.—United States.   5. Oral history.   I. Title.
KF390.O7N48 2009
344.73'09—dc22   2008053833

Printed in the United States of America
on acid-free paper

To Lucy Neuenschwander

| CONTENTS |

| PREFACE |

Oral history is everywhere. Today it seems as though there is virtually no area of American life that has not been visited by an oral historian. The range of practitioners extends from award-winning biographers to grade school children. Oral history is a research tool with virtually unlimited applications from the tens of thousands of veterans who have recorded their memories of America's wars courtesy of the Veterans History Project to the hundreds of authors who annually publish edited collections of interviews. A very selective listing of such books suggests that oral history has no subject matter boundaries:

What Was Asked of Us: An Oral History of the Iraq War by the Soldiers Who Fought It
Missing Pages: Black Journalists of Modern America: An Oral History
The Osama bin Laden I Know: An Oral History of al-Qaeda's Leader
The Other Hollywood: The Uncensored Oral History of the Porn Film Industry
Underground America: Narratives of Undocumented Lives

Despite such astronomical growth and the increasing public awareness of how oral histories enrich the historical record, there are still only a handful of reported court cases that address the legal issues that the practice of oral history can generate. This may not be the case for much longer. It is a truism in America that virtually any field of endeavor, whether in business or academia, that experiences rapid growth and increased public attention usually generates a growing number of legal challenges in the process. Many of these challenges may come from the increasingly contemporary subject matter emphasis of oral history research. In addition to the local historical society conducting oral histories with octogenarians, there are growing numbers of researchers who are studying subjects like illegal immigration, prostitution, AIDS, war crimes, and drug use. In this context, the advice given by attorney H. Mason Welch to oral historians attending the Fourth National Colloquium on Oral History in 1969 is still remarkably timely: "This occupation, like any other, harbors a possibility of inflicting real or imagined injury and wrongs upon others, and those things usually...result in litigation."

To address the potential legal concerns of oral historians, I wrote a short pamphlet entitled *Oral History and the Law* which the Oral History Association published in 1985. The foremost purpose of this pamphlet and the subsequent editions that followed in 1993 and 2002 was to identify and examine the potential legal issues facing oral historians and to suggest policies and procedures to avoid these problems. While this book shares the same goal, it represents a completely new and far more comprehensive examination of the myriad of legal concerns that go hand-in-hand with the practice of oral history in the 21st century. Readers, for example, will find numerous examples of exemplary practices and procedures drawn from a cross section of oral history programs to assist them in determining how best to deal with key legal issues. They will also encounter frequent discussions of professional ethics to aid them in laying a strong foundation upon which to erect the most legally sound policies and procedures. The recommended code of ethics for both oral historians and programs comes from the *Principles and Standards* of the Oral History Association. This code of ethics has also been incorporated into a checklist of questions entitled the *Oral History Evaluation Guidelines*. The intent of this code of ethics is to encourage those who gather, preserve, and utilize oral histories to do so in the most principled manner possible. Foremost among these obligations is the ethical treatment of interviewees. Although the OHA's *Principles and Standards/ Evaluation Guidelines* consists of statements of ethics that are not legally binding, the recommended practices that are set out provide a code of conduct which, if adhered to, lays a solid foundation for avoiding legal problems. Readers are also encouraged to read the entire *Principles and Standards/Evaluation Guidelines*, which appears in Appendix 2.

A Note on Legal Terms

The American legal system is often a mystery. Lawyers are like priests who engage in a system of court rituals and incantations that are frequently baffling to the everyday citizen. Whether a lawyer is appearing *pro hac vice* (a special appearance by a lawyer not licensed to practice in that jurisdiction) or making a motion *in limine* (an attempt to prevent evidence from being admitted), the legal terminology can seem impenetrable. Every effort has been made in this book to spare lay readers from having to grapple with excessively complex legal terminology. Where legal terms are utilized, a short definition of the word or phrase will always be provided.

The Use of State Cases

Throughout this book, the reader will also encounter many court cases. To enhance readability, only the names of the most important cases will appear in the text. Because there are very few cases dealing directly with oral history, most of the cases that are discussed in this book were chosen because they present factual situations that closely resemble what oral historians encounter. Except where noted, all cases discussed are published ones. In order for a case to be published in any state jurisdiction, it has to be decided by an appellate court and have precedential value. The latter term means that the legal holding of the case must be followed by lower courts within the state when they address the same issue.

The appellate courts in all fifty states have two primary responsibilities. The first is to review the work of the trial courts and either affirm their decisions or correct substantive errors. Their second responsibility is to establish legal precedents. This latter role is usually the province of the highest appellate court in a state. State legislatures can and often do preempt their highest court on matters of legal precedent by enacting laws. For example, a sizable number of the states have refused to recognize the privacy tort of false light discussed in Chapter 5. In Wisconsin, it was the legislature that decided to bar the filing of a lawsuit for false light in any state court. In other states, like Texas, it was the supreme court which determined that no lawsuit based on a claim of false light could be filed anywhere in the state.

A case with legal precedent in one state sometimes has a direct bearing on how the legal precedent on a particular issue is decided in another state. For example, *Hebrew Academy of San Francisco v. Goldman* is an important defamation case that was decided by the supreme court of California in 2007. The holding in the case provides binding precedent for all other courts in California. The impact of the decision in *Hebrew Academy* may, however, be persuasive to courts in other states for several reasons. First, it may be an issue that has not yet been addressed. Thus, an appellate court in such a state might find the California Supreme Court's ruling so convincing that they could decide to adopt it. If the highest appellate court in another state did so, then the legal holding in *Hebrew Academy* would in turn become a legal precedent in that jurisdiction. Another factor in the persuasiveness of a case is the standing of the court that issued the decision. Since California and New York probably hear more defamation cases than other jurisdictions, their decisions are bound to carry more weight.

The Use of Federal Cases

On the federal level, district courts are located in every state and conduct all of the trials. They also publish some of their decisions, unlike state trial courts. These decisions can and do serve as precedent if there is no appeal to the circuit court of appeal for that region. The thirteen regionally situated circuit courts serve as the primary appellate court on the federal level. Any decision that they publish serves as binding precedent for all of the district courts in that region. If the same issue subsequently arises in another circuit, the precedent established by any other circuit court of appeals is only persuasive and not binding.

Ideally, when there are legal precedents upon which different circuit courts of appeal disagree, the United States Supreme Court steps in to make the final ruling. Often, however, this does not happen because the vast majority of the cases that the Supreme Court takes are what are called discretionary appeals. In other words, the Supreme Court may choose not to weigh in on an issue that has produced conflicting legal precedents from different circuit courts. In recent years the Supreme Court has been taking fewer and fewer cases. On average, about ten thousand petitions for writ of certiorari (appeal requests) are filed annually with the Supreme Court. In 2007–2008, the high court agreed to hear fewer than one hundred of these cases. Given the Supreme Court's reluctance to take on a larger workload, rulings by the circuit courts of appeal have taken on even greater importance.

Prevention Is the Key

This preface would not be complete without emphasizing again that this book is first and foremost a venture in preventative or prophylactic law. As such, it is not a guide to successful litigation or a trial lawyer's handbook. The mission of the book is to help readers avoid legal controversy. The message that springs from every page is that legal problems are far less likely to occur if you establish sound procedures and policies and continually update them as needed.

Finally, this book is a general guide, does not constitute the practice of law, and should not be considered authoritative. It is intended to be a resource to assist non-lawyer and lawyer alike in gaining a sound understanding of the legal issues that oral historians should be most concerned about. By understanding the key legal issues that can arise, readers will be much better equipped to avoid becoming legally vulnerable. A local attorney who is licensed to practice law in your state or jurisdiction is always the best resource for the prevention and/or resolution of legal problems. My hope is that the material presented here will facilitate understanding of the key legal issues and enable readers to more clearly address them with a local attorney.

| ACKNOWLEDGMENTS |

Many of the suggestions offered to me in recent years by oral historians at conference sessions, by letter, and through exchanges on H-NET/OHA discussion list on oral history proved invaluable in the preparation of this book. I would like to thank all those who may have contributed in this manner for their valuable, if unknowing, assistance. I would also like to thank all of the oral historians and programs who responded to my request for sample legal release agreements. The numerous agreements that were sent in greatly enhanced my treatment of this vital legal area. Like any author, I am beholden to a number of key individuals without whose assistance I could not have completed this book. My friend Donald Ritchie not only provided me with incisive commentary on several chapters but also served as my sounding board throughout the preparation of this manuscript. Nancy Toff, my editor at Oxford, also deserves a great deal of credit. Her comments and suggestions were instrumental in making this legal work as germane and reader friendly as possible. My final acknowledgment goes to my wife Lucy. She was not only a constant source of encouragement and support but also provided invaluable assistance to her computer-challenged husband in the preparation of this work.

A GUIDE TO ORAL HISTORY
AND THE LAW

| | |

| 1 |

A Case Study

The vast majority of oral historians and programs have thus far managed to avoid spending any time in court. The case of *Society of Survivors of the Riga Ghetto, Inc. v. Huttenbach* is a notable exception to this generalization.[1] The litigation arose out of a contractual dispute between the leadership of the Society of Survivors of the Riga Ghetto and Dr. Henry R. Huttenbach, a professor of history at the City College of the City University of New York. During the late 1970s, the society began looking for a historian to write a history of the ghetto, which had been set up by the Nazis in the city of Riga, Latvia, during the period from 1941 to 1943. Since most of the material for such a work lay in the memories of survivors, the society wanted someone who would do the oral history interviews as well as the actual writing. They eventually chose Dr. Huttenbach, a recognized specialist in Holocaust studies. In preparation for writing the history, he interviewed more than one hundred survivors and collected a small archive of written material and memorabilia.

In 1982, the parties entered into their first written contract for the anticipated book, *The Holocaust in Riga: A History of the Riga Ghetto*. In addition to the monetary compensation that Huttenbach was to receive, he was to be listed as the author and have exclusive access to all archival materials until the manuscript was completed. Subsequent access by Huttenbach would be governed by the terms of an agreement between the society and Yad Vashem, the Holocaust museum in Jerusalem. The original contract specifically awarded copyright in the interviews Huttenbach conducted and the history he was writing to the society. After compiling a catalog of the archive, Huttenbach prepared and submitted a first draft of the book to the leaders of the society in the fall of 1984.

The cooperation and excellent progress that had characterized the begin-ning stages of this project quickly began to disappear once Huttenbach submit-ted the first draft. In early 1985, the leaders of the society began to take issue with the way in which Huttenbach was attempting to reconcile differing accounts among the survivors. The leadership also objected to a review article written by Professor Huttenbach which appeared in *The Voice of Auschwitz*. The article, which summarized the chapter describing the mass extermination of Jews in Salaspils, one of the concentration camps surrounding Riga, was written by Huttenbach to provide an advance notice for the forthcoming book. The leaders of the society, however, considered it to be an unauthorized publication. As the relationship between the parties soured, the society attempted to remove Huttenbach's name from the manuscript entirely. Once the parties had reached a complete impasse, the society filed a lawsuit in 1986 for breach of contract. The society demanded the return of all interviews and memorabilia in Huttenbach's possession as well as $100,000 in damages. Huttenbach counterclaimed for breach of contract and also sought monetary damages. Following a trial, the justice rendered what amounted to a plague-on-both-your-houses decision. She held that the copyright assignment contained in the original agreement was valid. The society as copyright owner, however, did not have the right to change drastically or revise the manuscript and still publish it bearing Huttenbach's name. Finally, both parties were permanently enjoined from publishing any part of the manuscript or using any of the interviews or materials gathered by Huttenbach without the express written permission of the other. The parties were to retain all materials in their respective possession, and the society was ordered to pay Professor Huttenbach the amount still owed from the original contract. In rendering this decision, the justice expressed her disappointment that a valuable research collection and historical work would not be made available to the public. From her vantage point, it was obvious from the attitude and demeanor of the litigants that there had been a total breakdown in the parties' relationship. The sad but realistic conclusion was that "the court can-not mandate cooperation between reluctant parties."[2]

What are the legal lessons to be learned from this case? To begin with, it is reassuring to see a court accept without question the ability to copyright oral history interviews. Questions occasionally have been raised about whether or not oral history interviews are indeed copyrightable. The case also points up the ines-capable fact that even the most legally sound and well-written agreements may not prevent the parties from having a falling-out and ending up in court. Legally sound procedures and policies will go a long way toward keeping oral historians and programs out of court, but as the *Huttenbach* case points up, there are no absolute guarantees.[3]

| 2 |

Legal Release Agreements

Americans live in a world that is ruled by legal agreements. The average American goes through life signing contractual agreements for credit cards, loans, insurance, and wireless service. To sell anything on eBay, one must first sign a legal agreement. Participants in organized road races must sign a legal agreement that basically waives the liability of the promoters should the runner be injured or suffer a heart attack. The vast majority of Americans usually sign these legal agreements without bothering to read the fine print. Even most lawyers rarely take the time to carefully read, let alone question the stock language that is found in consumer agreements. If an insurance agent or bank officer tells us we need to sign an agreement in order to receive coverage or a loan, the only question usually asked is, "Where do I sign?"

Against this backdrop, it is not surprising that while legal release agreements are essential to the effective functioning of any oral history program, they rarely receive the close attention that they deserve. The public debate surrounding the legal release agreement that former Supreme Court Justice Thurgood Marshall signed with the Library of Congress points up how a single ambiguous word can spell trouble.

Before he decided to donate his papers, including several oral histories, Justice Marshall made a highly unusual decision for a national public figure, namely that there should be immediate access to his papers after his death. This is precisely what happened in 1993. Some of his fellow Supreme Court justices and even members of Marshall's own family, however, did not take kindly to Marshall's decision. Before the furor subsided, a U.S. Senate subcommittee looked into the matter, and the Librarian of Congress was forced to publicly defend the agreement that Marshall signed.

The event that triggered this incident was a three-part series in the *Washington Post* beginning on May 23, 1993. The major focus of these articles was the inner workings of the Supreme Court. Some members of the Supreme Court, as well as members of Marshall's immediate family, were very uncomfortable with the personal characterizations and accounts of key court decisions that the *Post* was able to glean from the Marshall papers. Chief Justice William Rehnquist even wrote a letter to James Billington, the Librarian of Congress, in which he accused the library of "bad judgment" in allowing access to Marshall's papers so soon after his death.[1] He also warned that current justices might well decide to donate their papers to an archive other than the Library of Congress.

The focus of the inquiry by the Senate Subcommittee on Regulation and Government Information was whether or not the Library of Congress had abided by the terms of Marshall's agreement. After Marshall decided to deposit his papers at the Library of Congress in 1991, a deed of gift was drafted by the staff of the Library of Congress. The proposed agreement reflected his stated wish that there be immediate and unrestricted access to his papers. A cover letter invited him to make any changes he wished. He subsequently signed the agreement and returned it without making any changes. The key clause that prompted the Library of Congress to open his papers to researchers shortly after his death read, "Thereafter the collection shall be made available to the public at the discretion of the Library."[2] James Billington maintained that the library's discretion was purely technical in nature. All it amounted to was the time it would take the library staff to catalog the Marshall papers for public access. He noted that former justice William Douglas had also opted for immediate access. Critics of his decision, however, believed that the library's discretion was far broader and encompassed delaying access for a number of years.

Although the furor over the actions of the Library of Congress soon died down, Harry Blackmun, a colleague of Marshall's, sought to avoid a similar controversy by mandating that his papers could not be accessed until five years after his death.[3] The controversy surrounding the opening of the Marshall papers provides a useful segue to the importance of drafting legal release agreements that are legally binding and free of ambiguity.

DRAFTING LEGAL RELEASE AGREEMENTS

Although becoming increasingly rare, there still is an occasional posting on H-NET/OHA, the online discussion list for oral historians, by someone who is either just starting a program or in the process of revising an agreement and who would like to have copies of legal release agreements to use as drafting models. It is even easier to Google sample agreements by simply entering a phrase like "legal release agreements." While either method will certainly allow a program or individual to generate an agreement of some sort, there are far too many important legal and ethical issues that must be considered when putting together a release to take such an effortless approach. The best legal release agreements contain precise but not overly legalistic language, document the full meeting of the minds between the parties on all relevant issues, and provide a road map for future use and administration.[4] In other words, your agreement should be readily explainable to lay persons and defensible in court should such a challenge ever come to pass. Courts do not go out of their way to interpret contested agreements but when forced to do so generally apply fairly standard rules of construction. Although the deed of gift that Justice Marshall signed did not end up in court, if it had, the court would have treated it just like any other agreement that required interpretation to settle a dispute. To reach a definitive interpretation of the meaning of the "discretion" afforded the Library of Congress to make his papers available, a court would have considered evidence regarding Marshall's intent, the generally accepted meaning of the word in previous donor agreements, and the custom of the industry (i.e., preparation time for cataloging collections). At the very least, there would have been a lot of time and money spent on discovery and lawyers' fees. The resulting decision in turn might not have supported the limited interpretation of "discretion" that the Library of Congress invoked.

DEED OF GIFT AGREEMENTS

A deed of gift is the type of agreement that is most often used by oral historians to legally transfer the ownership of an interview. This choice is not surprising since there is a lengthy American philanthropic tradition of using such instruments to convey ownership of memorabilia and personal papers. Long before oral history came on the scene, archives and libraries relied primarily on deeds of gift to secure legal custody and the ability to utilize historical materials.[5] A gift is the voluntary transfer of property other than real estate while the donor is still alive. In most states, three elements must be met for the donation to qualify as a legal transfer: a clear intent to make the donation, actual delivery, and acceptance by the gift's recipient.[6] In an oral history setting, intent would be satisfied by the individual's willingness to either be interviewed or conduct an interview and then donate the resulting material. The elements of delivery and acceptance pose no difficulty as long as the recording and/or transcript are in the possession of the receiving entity.

To incorporate these elements into a legal release agreement, a simple sentence would suffice: "I herein permanently give, convey, and transfer my oral history to the Oral History Program." All three of the elements that make a deed of gift legally binding are obviously present in this sentence. Several sample deed of gift agreements appear in Appendix 1 (Nos. 1, 2, 5, 6, 7, and 8).

Contractual Agreements

Contract style agreements are also used by oral historians to secure the legal trans-fer of interviews but to a significantly lesser extent.[7] To qualify as an agreement that courts will recognize and enforce, a contract must contain four elements: agreement, consideration, competent parties, and a lawful objective.[8] Drafting an agreement that successfully incorporates these four elements is usually not a difficult task. A properly signed agreement that clearly identifies the respective parties and the interview to be transferred would certainly establish the agree-ment element. Consideration is more elusive but need not be. What it boils down to is the requirement that both parties actually give up something in the bargain. If an oral history program agrees to conduct an interview and then edit, possibly transcribe, and maintain the resulting version for future use, the time and money necessary to do so would most certainly qualify as consideration. Interviewees and interviewers are also investing considerable time and effort in addition to signing away their rights to the interview. Thus, both are giving up something. The last two elements, competent parties and legal object, are far removed from the work that oral historians do. The *Principles and Standards* of the Oral History Association cautions against the exploitation of interviewees. Any oral historian who would start or continue to interview an incompetent person would be acting far outside the ethical boundaries of professional ethics. The lawful objective element like-wise would only come into play if it could be shown that the real purpose of an interview was to defraud or misrepresent something. The likelihood that an oral historian would knowingly participate in such a scheme is inconceivable. Several sample contract style agreements (Nos. 3 and 4) appear in Appendix 1.

Prefatory Language

How does your legal release agreement begin? If yours is like most agreements, after the title at the top, the next line usually begins, "I, _____, herein perma-nently give, convey, and transfer to the Oral History Program. . . ." While there is nothing wrong with such an approach, inserting an opening paragraph to describe the work of the project, program, or individual researcher is advisable from both a legal and ethical standpoint. Legally speaking, a preface provides the overall context for the interviewee's decision to sign a release agreement. It also serves to reinforce the notion that the interviewee is part of a much larger historical undertaking. From an ethics standpoint, the first Responsibility to Interviewees listed in the OHA's *Principles and Standards* is to inform them "... of the purposes and procedures of oral history in general and of the aims and anticipated uses of the particular projects to which they are making their contributions."[9] The following is a good example of a context-setting preface:

> I, _____, am a participant in the Veterans History Project (hereinafter "VHP") of the Library of Congress American Folklife Center. I understand that the purpose of the VHP is to collect audio- and video-recorded oral histories of America's war veterans and of those who served in support of them, as well as selected related documentary materials such as photographs and manuscripts, for inclusion in the permanent collections of the Library of Congress. The oral histories and related materials serve as a record of American veterans' experiences and as a scholarly and educational resource for Congress and the general public.[10]

Future Use Clauses

During a workshop presentation at the Oral History Association's annual meeting, I asked if anyone had been forced to try and locate past interviewees to obtain consent to utilize their interviews in ways that were not envisioned in their original agreement. A number of those who raised their hands indicated that their decision to publish interviews on the Internet was what necessitated this effort. They went on to describe the difficulties in locating and contacting the interviewees and the even more daunting task of trying to track down family members for those interviewees who were deceased. The consensus among those who went through a reconsenting process was to pay special attention to the language that is inserted into the future use clause.

The ethical importance of fully informing the interviewee of all of the possible future uses to which his or her interview could be put is strongly underscored in the *Principles and Standards*. Five of the ten Responsibilities to Interviewees specifically address the issue of future use:

> 1. Interviewees should be informed of the purposes and procedures of oral history in general and the aims and anticipated uses of the particular projects to which they are making their contributions.

2. Interviewees should be informed of the mutual rights in the oral history process, such as editing, access restrictions, copyrights, prior use, royalties, and the expected disposition and dissemination of all forms of the record, including the potential for electronic distribution. . . .

4. Interviewers should guard against making promises to interviewees that the interviewers may not be able to fulfill, such as guarantees of publication and control over the use of interviews after they have been made public. In all future uses, however, good faith efforts should be made to honor the spirit of the interviewee's agreement. . . .

9. Given the rapid development of new technologies, interviewees should be informed of the wide range of potential uses of their interviews.

10. Good faith efforts should be made to ensure that the use of recordings and transcripts comply with both the letter and spirit of the interviewee's agreement.[11]

While there is some redundancy among these five Responsibilities, this simply underscores the great importance that the drafters of the *Principles and Standards* attached to full and complete disclosure.

But how does one craft a clause that is both ethically grounded and legally sound? There are three major ways in which programs and individuals have sought to effectively address this knotty issue:

1. *Broad, All Inclusive Language:* "For such scholarly or educational uses as the Oral History Program shall deem appropriate," or "The interview will be disseminated by the Oral History Program as it deems appropriate but not limited to, the exclusive right of reproduction, distribution, preparation of derivative works, public performance, and display."

2. *The Middle Ground:* "I understand that all materials produced from this interview, whether in tape, manuscript, electronic, film, digital or any other form, will be used only for research, educational, web, exhibition, program, presentation, and promotional purposes by the Oral History Program or its public."

3. *Listing Specific Potential Uses:* "Potential uses of the interviews (in whole or in part) include, but are not limited to incorporation in the following: an archive to be made available worldwide via digital networks, education curriculum, film or video documentaries, online computer websites, publications, disc based products, promotional or fundraising materials, and museum exhibits. In addition, interviews may be made available to other entities with similar educational or historical purposes."

While all four future use clauses would most likely be considered binding if challenged in court, the ethical dimension must also be given due consideration. If you juxtapose these four clauses against Responsibility No. 2, "Interviewees should be informed of . . . the expected disposition and dissemination of all forms of the record, including potential for electronic distribution," obviously, the latter two future use clauses do a much better job of satisfying this ethical mandate because of their greater specificity.

One last issue is the possibility that an archive or program may some day decide to utilize an interview for financial gain. The *Oral History Evaluation Guidelines* specifically addresses this issue and recommends that "interviewees are to be fully informed about the potential for and disposition of royalties that might accrue from the use of their interviews, including all forms of public pro-gramming"[12] This issue is rarely addressed in most release agreements because the prospect of financial gain is usually rather remote. When this is not the case, a simple clause can be used to address this possibility: "Unless otherwise specified below, I place no restrictions on noncommercial access to and use of my inter-views." An even stronger "not-for-profit" qualifier can also be inserted in future use clauses: "My interview cannot be used for any profit-making program or pub-lication without my express permission." While the likelihood of direct commer-cial exploitation by an archive or program is probably quite limited, in the event such an opportunity were to come along, this would certainly be an occasion for reconsenting.

Transfer of Copyright

Securing a specific assignment of an interviewee's and in some instances the inter-viewer's copyright interest is something that every legal release agreement should be drafted to do, for without that bundle of exclusive rights that make up copy-right (reproduction, distribution, display, public performance, and the creation of derivative works), subsequent use of any oral history interview would be severely limited. Even if you are one of those programs or individuals who dispense with copyright protection altogether by placing interviews into the public domain, you should include specific language in your legal release agreement to that effect.

The Copyright Act of 1976 specifically mandates that any transfer of copyright ownership must be in writing and signed by the owner to be valid.[13] Although the statute is silent on whether inclusion of the word copyright is actu-ally required for a valid transfer of ownership, leaving it out serves no purpose. As the Court of Appeals for the Ninth Circuit noted, a writing transferring copyright ownership ". . . doesn't have to be a Magna Charta; a one-line pro forma statement will do."[14] Furthermore, according to the same Circuit Court in another decision, no magic words must be included to satisfy the statute.[15] Thus, language such as "I transfer to the Oral History Program legal title and all literary property rights to my interviews, including copyright" is quite sufficient.

Nonexclusive Licenses for Interviewees?

Interviewees obviously come from many different backgrounds. For most, receiving a copy of the recording and/or transcript officially ends the process. Not all interviewees follow this path. For some, the oral history experience inspires them to embark upon their own family or community history project. This effort may even result in some sort of publication. The easiest way to allow for this possibility is for the sponsoring program to grant a nonexclusive license to interviewees to allow them to utilize their interviews during their lifetime. Such a license does not place any constraints on the program's or archive's ownership and future use of the copyright to an interview. The granting of such a license can be achieved by inserting a simple clause into a legal release agreement: "This gift does not preclude any use that I may wish to make during my lifetime of my interview, including publication."

Restricting, Sealing, and Masking Identity

A significant number of oral history programs routinely provide interviewees with the opportunity to restrict access, seal their interviews for a given period of time, or mask their identity. Although some programs use a separate release agreement to accomplish this, most programs simply include a section in their regular agreement where such restrictions can be documented. In the latter type of agreements, a checklist is usually provided listing the types of access limitations available with appropriate space for the specifics to be set forth. Other agreements have a more open-ended recital: "Access to and use of my interviews is subject to the following restrictions: _____."

What is often left out of such restriction is any language that informs the interviewee that the program or archive cannot guarantee that the restriction will be upheld under all circumstances. If someone were to file a freedom of information request (known as FOIA, for the Freedom of Information Act) for an interview held by a state supported program or serve a subpoena, the best that any repository can do is to mount a reasonable defense. Although the prospect that a restricted interview might be the subject of either an FOIA request or a subpoena is very remote, it is both ethically and legally advisable to include some sort of cautionary language like, "The Oral History Program agrees to take all reasonable steps to maintain the confidentiality of your interviews pursuant the restrictions you imposed. The Program cannot fully guarantee that it will be able to prevent access in the face of a FOIA request or a subpoena from a court of competent jurisdiction."

The ethical reference to this issue comes from two questions on the OHA's *Evaluation Guidelines* checklist. The first question asks whether "interviewees understand their rights . . . to seal portions of the interviews, or in extremely sensitive circumstances even to remain anonymous?" The second question asks whether "All prior agreements made with interviewees are honored?"[16] Legally, even with a specific *caveat* clause, there would be a responsibility for the repository to raise more than a token defense to an FOIA request or a subpoena. Whether most programs that offer to restrict interviews have a contingency plan in place to address such challenges is unclear. For example, where would the lawyer come from to mount a defense, to say nothing of the funds to pay for such services?

Warranty Clauses

A warranty is nothing more than "a promise that a proposition of fact is true."[17] In other words, it is exactly what it is represented to be. A very small number of oral history programs include an interviewee warranty clause in their legal release agreements.[18] The purpose of such a clause is to protect against an interviewee who previously gave similar interviews and assigned the rights to them to somebody else: "I herein warrant that I have not already assigned or in any way encumbered or impaired any of the aforementioned rights in my memoir." There is really very little need for such a clause unless an oral history program is interviewing high profile individuals who would be the most likely candidates for repeat interviews.

Indemnity Clauses

If you have ever run or ridden your bicycle in a nonprofit road race or event, more than likely you were required to sign a form that released the sponsors from any liability if you were injured, became ill, or even died. An indemnity clause often starts off with a release of liability but goes on to place the responsibility for any future medical, litigation, and settlement costs upon the party who agrees to shoulder this burden. In effect, an indemnity clause absolves someone of his or her negligence. While most oral history programs do not include such clauses in their agreements, the few that do seek to protect themselves from liability for any future misuse of interviews: "I release and indemnify the Oral History Program from any and all claims arising out of or in connection with the use of the interview, including but not limited to any claims of defamation, copyright violation, invasion of privacy, or right of publicity."

If enforceable, such a clause might seem to be a wise precaution for an archive or program to implement. Enforceability, however, is the major problem. The general rule is that indemnity clauses are not favored in the law and will be strictly construed by a reviewing court.[19] Basically, if one party to a contract is going to shoulder sole responsibility for the other party's negligence, courts want to make extra sure that it was something that was actually bargained for and clearly understood. To that end, courts will scrutinize the language of the clause, and the relative standing of the parties, and will even consider whether a lay person could understand what he or she was signing away.[20]

The careful reader has already picked up on the major problem in all this. If a program's legal release agreement is a deed of gift, the bargaining process that applies to contracts is really not present. There is no exchange of consideration between the oral history program and the interviewee. While certain terms in a deed of gift may be subject to negotiation, the bargaining process that is central to all contracts is generally not. Thus, an indemnity clause that is located in a deed of gift agreement would be, to say the least, a fish out of water. But for the sake of this discussion, let us presume that the indemnity clause at issue is in a contract-style release agreement. If an interviewee who is facing the burden of defending against a lawsuit arising out of his or her interview challenges the validity of an indemnity clause, the reviewing court would most likely look closely at a number of issues. The first would be how the clause was presented prior to the signing of the agreement. A second consideration would be the relative bargaining position of the parties and whether the clause was unreasonably favorable to the party who advocated it.

If there was scant discussion of the clause and the interviewee did not actively negotiate the terms of the legal release agreement, the indemnity clause at issue would appear at the very least to be one-sided and at the very worst an unconscionable benefit to the drafting party. Since in most oral history situations it is the program which invites someone to be interviewed and the interviewees only tangible benefit is a copy of the recording and/or transcript and perhaps a nonexclusive license, asking them to agree in return to foot the bill for any legal problems that arise from the future use of their interviews would hardly signal a level playing field. Unconscionable contract clauses are those that affront decency and shock the conscience; indemnity clauses, however well intended, would seem to be prime candidates for such a designation, which would in turn render them unenforceable.[21]

The most prominent user of indemnity clauses for both interviewees and interviewers is the Veterans History Project. Perhaps because it has already produced more than fifty-eight thousand interviews and is so nationally prominent, its use of such clauses has encouraged other programs to follow suit. The release agreement that the American Folklife Center at the Library of Congress uses for all interviews is not labeled a deed of gift nor does it include standard gifting language except for frequent recitals that begin with "I hereby grant to the Library of Congress ownership. . . ." It is also definitely not a contract style type of agreement.

The nature of the agreement is less important, however, than how the American Folklife Center processes the thousands of interviews it receives annually. Unlike the vast majority of oral history programs, the recordings are not listened to or reviewed prior to being cataloged and placed in the appropriate collection. This hands-off approach explains why the indemnity clause was inserted into the release agreements in the first instance. The purpose was to shift all liability for future use to the submitters. There is no negligence to be excused here because the American Folklife Center makes the interviews available without any content review. Since the American Folklife Center, unlike most oral history programs, never places an inquiring eye on the interviews it takes in, the indemnity clause in their agreements is somewhat more understandable. Nevertheless, because their forms are part of an online kit, there would still be a real question as to whether the veteran and his or her interviewer were properly apprised of this potentially huge liability.

The ethics of such clauses are not specifically addressed in OHA's *Evaluation Guidelines* but are doubtless covered by the checklist item "Interviewees are provided a full and easily comprehensible explanation of their legal rights before being asked to sign a contract or deed of gift transferring rights, title, and interest in the tape(s) and transcript(s)...."[22] If after reading this discussion of indemnity clauses you plan to continue or even start using one, it is crucial that you document the process by which you alert an interviewee to this risk-shifting provision. The more direct and full your disclosure, the better chance such a clause may hold up if ever challenged.

Right of Publicity Clauses

The right of publicity essentially protects individuals from the use of their name or likeness for commercial gain without their express permission. It is a privacy interest that everyone has but is most often identified with movie stars and sports figures. Although the law is unclear on whether the right of publicity can be violated if the unauthorized use is nonprofit in nature, Responsibility No. 7 of the *Principles and Standards* cautions against the "possible exploitation of interviewees."[23] Using an interviewee's likeness or name to promote a commercial program or publication without specific approval would certainly impinge on his or her right of publicity. To do so for some nonprofit venture might not violate the right of publicity from a legal standpoint but would be clearly unethical. To avoid the problem of having to go back to a narrator years after he or she was interviewed, a few programs and archives have inserted a right of publicity release into their standard agreements: "I agree that my name and/or likeness may be used to promote programs and publications of the Oral History Project."

LEGAL RELEASE AGREEMENTS FOR INTERVIEWERS

There is already considerable evidence that supports the position that an interviewer is a joint author of an interview for copyright purposes. The internal policies of the United States Copyright Office mandate that when a registration application for an oral history interview only names one of the parties (interviewer or interviewee) as the author, the staff is to seek further clarification before completing the registration. This administrative position is grounded on the assumption that "a work consisting of an interview often contains copyrightable authorship by the person interviewed and the interviewer. Each owns the expression in the absence of an agreement to the contrary."[24] The Veterans History Project also treats the interviewer as a joint author. Its online interview kit includes legal release agreements for both the veteran and the interviewer, and for an interview to be accepted, it must be accompanied by a signed release from both. Although this is not yet black letter law, to eliminate any uncertainty, the standard practice should be to have all interviewers who are not full-time employees of a program or archive, including volunteers, sign a release agreement for every interview that they conduct. Employees do not need to sign an interviewer release because any copyright interest that they might have in an interview passes directly to their employer under the work-made-for-hire doctrine. Sample release agreements for interviewers (Nos. 5, 6, and 7) can be found in Appendix 1.

IRB MODIFIED AGREEMENTS

For practitioners of oral history who are based on college or university campuses or at medical facilities, legal release agreements more than likely will have to win the approval of an Institutional Review Board (IRB). Despite continuing efforts by the Oral History and American Historical Associations to exclude oral history research from IRB oversight, at most colleges and universities, even student oral history projects are reviewed by an IRB. The legal release agreement is usually at the center of such reviews. Under the Common Rule, consent is the most important consideration in determining whether a human subject has agreed to participate in a trial or study.[25] Most IRBs spend a good deal of their deliberations making sure that the consent procedure for a particular study satisfies the eight elements for consent. In most of the legal release agreements that have received IRB approval, the following six elements for consent are present:

1. a statement of the purpose of the research, duration of participation and description of the procedure to be used;

2. a statement of foreseeable risks if any;
3. a statement of foreseeable benefits to the individual or in general;
4. a statement indicating that the participation was voluntary and could be terminated at any time without penalty;
5. a statement of confidentiality if applicable;
6. a contact person or persons should an interviewee have questions or concerns.[26]

The following agreement demonstrates how these six consent elements can be directly incorporated into an oral history release:

> The interview will be conducted in the form of a guided conversation and will last approximately_____. I will be free to decline to answer any question that makes me uncomfortable. Moreover, I have the right to stop the recording at any time with no negative consequences. There are no foreseeable risks in doing this interview. The benefit of the interview is to the general public in the form of increased historical knowledge. I recognize that because the interview will be donated to the University of_____ there is no assumption of confidentiality unless I expressly request it.

The final element, whom to contact with questions or concerns, usually appears at the bottom of the consent page and includes the project and the human research protection program's office phone numbers and e-mail addresses. For most oral historians, having to obtain consent by first walking potential narrators through a kind of horror chamber of risks is nothing short of overkill. However, the *Principles and Standards* of the OHA actually mirrors some of these consenting elements. Responsibility No. 7 cautions: "Interviewers should guard against possible exploitation of interviewees and be sensitive to the ways in which their interviews might be used. Interviewers must respect the rights of interviewees to refuse to discuss certain subjects...."[27] Two sample IRB modified agreements (Nos. 9 and 10) appear in Appendix 1.

LEGAL RELEASE AGREEMENTS FOR K–1 2 PROJECTS

Thousands of teachers on all levels use oral history in their teaching. Most of these teachers see oral history as just another teaching resource, a tool much like a field trip or computer program. Quite naturally, most of these teachers do not belong to national, regional, or even local oral history groups, nor do they generally attend conferences or seminars put on by such groups. Although they may be hard to count, there is no doubt that these "silent users" are definitely out there.

The major pedagogical consideration for most K–12 teachers who occasionally have students conduct interviews is to enrich course content. Thus, a unit on the Great Depression or the Vietnam War can have far more impact if students are able to interview someone who actually experienced it. In such situations, the training that students receive is often heavily weighted toward interviewing. Preserving, archiving, and making such interviews available for future classroom use are usually well beyond the scope of the project. There are, to be sure, a handful of middle schools and high schools, such as the D.C. Everest Schools in Wausau, Wisconsin, that have developed nationally recognized oral history programs in which student interviews generate publications and media productions. These are not the norm.

Experts on school-based oral history projects advocate the use of legal release agreements for all projects.[28] They point out the usual areas for legal concern such as defamation and copyright infringement and recommend a safe-rather-than-sorry approach. There is much to be said for such an approach especially if the interviews will indeed be kept and utilized in the future. But if this is not the case, something less than a full-blown deed of gift or contract is more advisable. A simple one-time permission-to-use agreement is all that is really necessary. Such an agreement dispenses with all assignments of rights and future use clauses; it focuses solely on the intended classroom use. It also leaves no ambiguity as to what happens to the recording or video after the unit is finished: "Once the project is completed the recordings of my interview, as well as any transcript, will be returned to me. No copies of my interview shall be retained by the student interviewer, teacher, or school without my express permission." A final sentence or two can be inserted to affirm that the interviewee's copyright interest in his or her interview has not been disturbed or altered by signing this permission-to-use agreement. In the end, students using permission-to-use agreements will still learn about how the law applies to and protects the spoken history. A sample permission-to-use agreement appears in Appendix 1 (No. 11).

Explaining Legal Release Agreements

When and how a program or archive presents a legal release agreement to an interviewee and/or interviewer for signing is really an administrative, not a legal, issue. Although there is no one best method or procedure, the explanation process should not be rushed or short-circuited because of the fear that too much discussion of legal issues may dissuade someone from signing. In other words, an expedited approach is not recommended. It is a rare person in today's world who does not enter into legal agreements, whether to borrow money, buy a car, hire a roofer, or sign up for a credit card. This being the case, securing the interviewee's or interviewer's informed consent should be viewed as an important educational process and not just a *pro forma* exercise. By carefully walking potential signees through their agreements, the prospect of future misunderstandings can be significantly reduced, and the interviewee may provide even better interviews because of his or her understanding of the legal boundaries. The latter consideration is aptly explained by Linda Shopes, one of the leading advocates for professional conduct by oral historians: "An interviewee who understands the purpose of the interview, who knows he or she is speaking for the record, can measure comments about another person. A conscientious interviewer can avoid setting up too intimate an exchange, one that nurtures imprudent confidences."[29]

CONCLUSION

Legal release agreements are vital tools for oral historians. As such, they should be carefully drafted from the start and reexamined periodically to determine whether they are in need of revision or expansion. Such reexamination can be greatly minimized if the initial creation process was done with an eye toward drafting an agreement that is grounded on professional ethics and accurately reflects the law of binding agreements in the appropriate jurisdiction. Although there is no perfect agreement, those that have been thoughtfully drafted, receive the input of a knowledgeable local attorney, and are periodically revisited are the most likely to be trouble free.

| 3 |

Compelled Release of Interviews

Subpoenas and FOIA Requests

ORAL HISTORY AS EVIDENCE

In the eyes of a court, either state or federal, a recording or transcript of an oral history interview is hearsay. Although there are numerous exceptions to the rules of evidence that bar the introduction of hearsay evidence, none of these exceptions usually apply to the out-of-court statements that are made by an interviewee in the course of an oral history interview. The primary means by which oral history does make it into court is through the opinion testimony of expert witnesses.[1] Rule 703 of the Federal Rules of Evidence provides that an expert witness may rely upon inadmissible evidence "if of a type reasonably relied upon by experts in the particular field in forming opinions and inferences upon a subject, . . ."[2] While state rules of evidence vary somewhat from the Federal Rules of Evidence, there are provisions in most state evidence codes for similar reliance by experts on hearsay evidence such as oral history. Under Rule 703, a trial judge does have the authority to exclude an expert's testimony if the court determines that the hearsay evidence upon which he or she is basing his opinion is not the type of evidence that can be "reasonably relied upon," but such authority is rarely exercised.

In litigation involving Native American land or tribal rights claims, for example, oral tradition is usually seen as a type of hearsay that can be "reasonably relied upon" by an expert in offering an opinion on the authenticity of such claims. As noted by the Court of Appeals for the Ninth Circuit in a 1998 case, *Cree v. Flores,* "were it otherwise, the history and culture of a society that relies on oral history tradition could be brought before the fact finder only with the greatest of difficulty and probably with less reliability."[3] In this case, the Yakima Indian Nation filed suit against Washington State officials to prevent them from collecting truck license and overweight permit fees from Indian drivers who hauled timber from tribal lands to outside purchasers. Since the Yakima maintained that an 1855 treaty exempted them from such fees, the court battle was largely between dueling experts. One of the experts for the State of Washington was a history professor from Central Washington University who had written a biography of Isaac J. Stevens, the territorial governor of Washington at the time the treaty was signed. The chief expert for the Yakima was William Yallup, a tribal member who was well versed in Yakima history and culture. After losing at the trial level, the State of Washington appealed. One of its major issues on appeal was the decision by the trial court to give more credence to Yallup's testimony than that of the experts for the state. Attorneys for the state questioned the trustworthiness of oral tradition as the primary basis for an expert's testimony. They cited ample legal precedents for their position that when there are dueling experts, the ones who rely on oral tradition to formulate an opinion are in general less reliable than the experts who do not. The Ninth Circuit, however, upheld the both the district court's decision to rely more heavily on Yallup's testimony as well as the judgment in favor of the Yakima.

Oral History and Discovery

If oral history cannot come into a court proceeding on its own, why would an attorney even bother trying to get his or her hands on sealed or restricted interview material? The simple answer is discovery. This is the pretrial evidence-gathering process that precedes all criminal and civil cases. During this sometimes lengthy period between the filing of a civil lawsuit or the beginning of a criminal proceeding and the actual trial, both sides amass as much evidence as time and money will allow them to determine if they will have the upper hand if the matter goes to trial. According to one authority on civil litigation, "Discovery is very, very broad.... As a practical matter almost anything goes. For this reason, the parties are permitted to go on fishing expeditions to discover virtually anything they want."[4] So even though oral history may be hearsay, if there is even a remote chance that interviews might be helpful, attorneys will usually want to take a look rather than miss any valuable evidence.

At this writing, only a tiny handful of oral history programs have ever been either threatened with a subpoena let alone served with one. The ability of oral history programs to remain so untouched by the discovery requests of lawyers is not likely to continue. The best indicators that more subpoenas will be forthcoming are first, the increasingly contemporaneous subject matter focus of many oral his-torians. The second is closely tied to the first, namely the exploration of more and more controversial topics. This tendency is borne out by the increasing number of programs that are allowing interviewees to restrict or seal their interviews or to remain anonymous.[5] Stock clauses like "No researcher shall be allowed access to my interview without my written permission," and "My interview will remain closed to all researchers until _____ or my death, whichever occurs first," are increasingly present in legal agreements utilized by a wide variety of programs.

THREE ILLUSTRATIVE CASES

A Murder Trial

A murder trial in Mississippi involving the Imperial Wizard of the White Knights of the Ku Klux Klan, a violent offshoot of the KKK, provides a dramatic example of how and why a prosecutor considered the discovery of oral history interviews to be a potentially important part of his case. In 1966, Vernon Dahmer, a black civil rights leader, died after his home was firebombed by members of the White Knights. During the intervening years, Samuel H. Bowers, the Imperial Wizard of the White Knights, was tried four different times for arson and the murder of Dahmer. All four trials ended in mistrials because all-white juries could not agree on a verdict. Finally, in August 1998, a jury found Bowers guilty of the firebomb-ing and murder of Dahmer, and he was sentenced to life in prison.

Prior to the final trial, the district attorney subpoenaed three oral his-tory interviews with Bowers that were housed in the Mississippi Department of Archives and Records. The interviews were part of a larger project on the civil rights movement in Mississippi. At Bowers's request, no one could access his interviews without his written permission.[6] Attorneys for the Department of Archives and Records sought a protective court order to prevent the unseal-ing of the Bowers interviews. They argued that the subpoena represented third party interference with the agreement between the archives and Bowers. They also warned that breaching this agreement would have a chilling effect on future interviewees. Their motion for a protective order was denied, however, because such an order would have unduly restrained the ability of the court to con-sider relevant evidence. As a result, the transcripts of his three interviews were turned over to the district attorney. Although the interviews were not actually used in Bowers's trial because he did not take the stand in his own defense, the prosecution was prepared to use material from the interviews to impeach his testimony.

An Arson Investigation

The next case also involved a criminal prosecution, but in this instance the materials sought for discovery were not sealed or restricted interviews but the research notes of a graduate student. In the early 1980s, Mario Brajuha was a graduate student at the State University of New York at Stony Brook doing ethnographic research for his dissertation, "The Sociology of the American Restaurant." He conducted a substantial part of his research by working as a waiter at several Long Island restaurants. In addition to using direct observation, he also interviewed a number of his coworkers. Although he did not tape record them, he did keep detailed field notes of their comments and observations. Shortly after a fire of unknown origin destroyed one of the restaurants he worked at, a local prosecutor, suspecting arson, interviewed Brajuha. Though he freely discussed what he knew from personal observation, he refused to turn over his field notes to the prosecutor. After the prosecutor served Brajuha with a subpoena, a lengthy legal battle ensued. It was finally resolved when the Court of Appeals for the Second Circuit ordered a partial disclosure of his field notes while allowing him to redact sensitive materials that were not relevant to the arson investigation.[7] The court refused, however, to recognize the "scholar's" privilege Brajuha's attorneys requested to try to shield his research from any discovery. In the wake of his subpoena fight, he found that there was a substantial drop-off in the willingness of fellow restaurant workers to talk with him.

A Criminal Damage Investigation

The third case also centered on oral communications received by a graduate student in sociology. In this instance, however, the doctoral candidate was unable to secure any protection from the court. The focus of James Richard Scarce's research was the radical environmental movement. He had published a book on the subject in 1990 entitled *Eco-Warriors: Understanding the Radical Environmental Movement*. In August 1991, someone broke into the animal research facility at Washington State University. The intruders did over $100,000 in damage. Through its spokesperson, Rodney Coronado, a group called the Animal Liberation Front (ALF) claimed responsibility. In the course of their investigation, the police learned that Coronado had been house-sitting for Scarce in the weeks prior to the vandalism. They also determined that Scarce and Coronado had discussed the break-in shortly after it occurred. As a result, Scarce and his wife were ordered to appear before a grand jury that was to determine whether charges would be filed. Scarce, however, refused to answer any questions regarding his conversations with Coronado or any other members of the ALF. In doing so, he maintained it was his "scholar's" privilege not to answer. This privilege, he maintained, was derived from the First

Amendment and federal common law. Although his lawyers referenced several cases including Brajuha's, in which a court had recognized some limits on discovery when a scholar's research was at issue, the Court of Appeals for the Ninth Circuit ruled that no court "... has actually recognized a scholar's privilege to withhold from a federal grand jury confidentially obtained information which is relevant to a legitimate grand jury inquiry and is sought in good faith."[8] When Scarce refused to relent, he was found to be in contempt of court and ended up serving 153 days in jail.

Is There a Scholar's Privilege?

Both Mario Brajuha and James Richard Scarce asked courts to recognize a "scholar's" or "researcher's" privilege. In both instances they were unsuccessful. At this writing only the Seventh Circuit Court of Appeals has been willing to recognize a qualified "scholar's" privilege. But this recognition has been limited to civil (not criminal) litigation, and its primary goal is to prevent premature disclosure of research that might jeopardize either completion of an advanced degree or the economic benefit from future publication.[9] To secure the benefit of this qualified privilege in the Seventh Circuit, a scholar or graduate student whose research has been subpoenaed still has to make a proper showing. The task of making such a showing is almost certain to be very time-consuming and costly.

Is There an Archival Privilege?

The Bowers case was the only one of the previous three cases in which the subpoena was served upon an archive rather than an individual researcher. Obviously, the Mississippi Department of Archives and Records' effort to prevent access to its interviews was unsuccessful. One possible avenue of defense that its attorneys did not pursue was to request the creation of an "archival" privilege. This is essentially the same as the "scholar's" privilege but would protect a library or archive from having to turn over sealed or restricted materials in response to a subpoena. The most extended treatment of this privilege comes from a case that directly involved archival material.

Beginning in 1966, Anne Braden began donating her papers to the State Historical Society of Wisconsin. The papers, which eventually totaled 240 boxes, documented the thirty years that she and her husband spent as civil rights activists and her leadership role in the National Committee Against

Repressive Legislation (NCARL). In the early 1980s, NCARL and other civil rights groups sued the FBI for monetary damages to compensate them for years of harassment, illegal surveillance, and covert break-ins (black bag jobs.).[10] After learning that the Braden papers were at the State Historical Society of Wisconsin, lawyers for the FBI secured a subpoena to inspect the papers for evidence that might be of assistance in defending against this lawsuit. Because the papers could only be accessed with Braden's permission, the historical society refused to comply with the subpoena. One of the main defenses raised by Braden and the historical society in the court proceeding that followed was to ask the judge to create an "archival" privilege. Such a privilege, they argued, was necessary because many prominent individuals would be deterred from donating their papers if restrictions on access and use could be brushed aside by a subpoena. Such action would also have a negative impact on the free flow of ideas and scholarship in general if fewer collections of personal papers were available to researchers.

Unfortunately for Braden and the historical society, the court was not persuaded either by this argument or her attempt to ground such a privilege on the few cases in which courts had been willing to offer a limited degree of protection to academic researchers facing very expansive subpoenas. The latter effort, which has been tried in several subsequent cases, has failed repeatedly because no clear-cut "scholar's" privilege has ever been endorsed by any federal or state court. As one court categorically noted, "Non-retained or involuntary experts or researchers do not have any federal statutory, case law or common law privilege which protects against their having to involuntarily share their expertise with parties in the litigation."[11] Without a "scholar's" privilege to build on, it is simply unrealistic to expect that any court in the future will agree to carve out a wholly novel "archival" privilege.[12]

INFORMING INTERVIEWEES THAT RESTRICTIONS ARE NOT ABSOLUTES

Collectively, these four cases simply acknowledge the long-standing principle that the public, through the courts, has a right to every person's evidence unless there is a recognized privilege to the contrary. Since there are no generally recognized protective privileges for scholars or archives, oral historians who receive subpoenas for restricted interviews are left with the same possible defenses and remedies that any citizen or group has, namely, trying to quash or limit the scope of the subpoena on the grounds that the scope is overly broad; the subpoena seeks material that is only marginally relevant; or the cost (time and money) of producing the materials to the holder is out of proportion to the perceived need.

The increasing utilization of academic researchers as experts in recent years, especially in civil cases, suggests that this greater reliance on academicians for evidence may make more lawyers inclined to try to bring in research materials via subpoena.[13] If this occurs, both oral history archives and researchers utilizing oral history need to be more aware of this prospect. They in turn have a professional obligation to make sure those interviewees who request and are granted the right to seal or restrict access to their interviews understand that such clauses are not absolutes. Such a disclosure would be in keeping with the *Principles and Standards* of the Oral History Association: "Interviewers should guard against making promises to interviewees that the interviewers may not be able to fulfill, such as guarantees of publication and control over the use of interviews after they have been made public."[14] If this advice is read in conjunction with the responsibility to respect the rights of interviewees "to restrict access to the interview, or, under extreme circumstances, even to choose anonymity . . . ," the mandate becomes even clearer.[15] The *Principles and Standards* would thus seem to recommend that a clear warning about the legal limits of any seal, restriction, or promise of confidentiality via anonymity be given to those interviewees who opt for such restrictions.

Before rushing off to end or sharply curtail the practice of sealing or restricting interviews, consider several options. The first is to simply share with interviewees who wish to restrict their interviews the remote but still real prospect that a seal or restriction may not prevent court access. This need not alarm or frighten a potential interviewee if it is handled properly. There need not be any speculative discussion about why a party to a lawsuit might even want to examine the sealed or restricted interview materials. Obviously, only interviews which discuss more contemporaneous or controversial subjects or persons would be the ones that would be most likely to draw the attention of a party to a lawsuit. There is also the question of who would bear the costs in the event that a legal battle developed over access to sealed or restricted interviews. Adding some language that clarifies who will mount a legal defense should this be necessary is a sound idea: "The Oral History Program will defend your access restriction against any legal challenge."

CERTIFICATES OF CONFIDENTIALITY

Oral historians at colleges and universities may apply to their Institutional Review Board (IRB) to obtain a certificate of confidentiality. Such certificates allow a researcher to fend off every possible type of subpoena and open records request ". . . from all persons not connected with the conduct of such research for the names and other identifying characteristics of such individuals."[16] The federal agency that sponsors these certificates, the National Institute of Health (NIH), claims that such certificates "... allow the investigator and others who have access to research records to refuse to disclose identifying information on research participants in any civil, criminal, administrative, legislative, or other proceeding, whether at the federal, state or local level."[17] The oral history researchers who might benefit the most from such a protective shield are the ones who focus on drug or alcohol abuse, mental health, and illegal behavior. For example, an oral history project in Collin County, Texas, on the life histories of recent immigrants was granted a Certificate of Confidentiality by the university IRB. Given the increased attempts to ferret out and prosecute illegal immigrants, the project director obviously deemed the certificate an important safeguard.[18] It is important to note, however, that such certificates protect only the identity of participants in a study and not the research data. They also only offer protection during the period of time when the study is considered active. Finally, there are no court cases that directly support the NIH's claim that the certificates will prevent all unwanted legal intervention.

ADMISSIBILITY BY STATUTE

Despite the general prohibition against oral histories being used directly in court, except through the mouth of an expert, the Native American Graves Protection and Repatriation Act (NAGPRA), passed in 1990, specifically mandates that oral tradition (oral history) can be used by tribes seeking to repatriate remains or sacred objects. The most dramatic application of this evidentiary mandate was in a case that determined whether a group of tribes or government scientists should have possession and control over the Kennewick Man, the nine-thousand-year-old skeletal remains discovered in 1996 along the banks of the Columbia River outside Kennewick, Washington. Prior to the court battle, the U. S. Department of the Interior hired Daniel Boxberger, an anthropologist at the University of Western Washington, to determine whether oral tradition did in fact establish the requisite "cultural affinity" between the tribes and the Kennewick Man. Based primarily on Boxberger's findings, since most other types of viable evidence were lacking, the secretary of the interior concluded that "collected oral tradition evidence suggests a continuity between the cultural group represented by the Kennewick remains and the modern-day claimant Indian Tribes."[19] A group of government scientists subsequently challenged the secretary's determination and were successful primarily because the court found the heavy reliance on oral narratives spanning more than 8500 years to be highly problematic. The tribes and the secretary in turn appealed to the Ninth Circuit Court of Appeals. In affirming the trial court, the Ninth Circuit also focused on the evidentiary problems with the oral tradition evidence: "Because the value of such accounts is limited by concerns of authenticity, reliability, and accuracy, and because the record as a whole does not show where history or real fact ends and mythic tale begins, we do not think that the oral traditions of interest to Dr. Boxberger were adequate to show the required significant relation of the Kennewick Man's remains to the Tribal Claimants."[20]

In general, however, Native American groups have been able to effectively use oral tradition and oral history evidence in NAGPRA proceedings and also in other instances in which federal statutes require agencies to consider, and in some cases actually conduct, interviews to determine whether past religious or cultural practices would preclude a particular land use. In a 2007 case, the Navajo Nation was able to temporarily stop a ski resort from using treated wastewater to make snow on land that oral histories helped to establish was vital to the Navajo religion.[21]

SPECIAL HEARINGS AND PROCEEDINGS

There are also instances in which the rules of evidence are either relaxed or do not apply. One such instance involved a final hearing in Federal Claims Court to determine whether a settlement agreement between the federal government and Japanese-Latin Americans who had been interned in Peru during World War II would be approved. Grace Shimizu, the coordinator of the Japanese Peruvian Oral History Project, gave direct testimony to the court regarding the fifty interviews she had conducted, and five of the interviewees also testified about their experiences. Ultimately, the financial settlement was approved by the court.[22]

FREEDOM OF INFORMATION REQUESTS

Oral history programs that are operated by federal or state entities face an additional challenge to any sealed or restricted interviews in the form of Freedom of Information Act (FOIA) or open records requests. All fifty states as well as the federal government have such statutes, whose sole purpose is to afford the public broad access to governmental records.[23] For any record to be exempted from an FOIA request, it must fit into a statutorily created exemption. The burden of establishing that certain information is exempt from an open records request falls upon the shoulders of the agency that possesses the record. When called upon to resolve a dispute over a claimed exemption, courts are to apply the narrowest definition possible to the exemptions at issue.

Litigation involving some post-9/11 oral history interviews provides a good case study of the reach of open records laws. In addition to a number of other oral history projects that sought to preserve the memories of survivors and rescuers after 9/11, the New York City Fire Department (FDNY) launched its own internal oral history project. A reporter for the *New York Times* subsequently filed an open records request to access the 511 interviews that had been completed up to that time. When the FDNY denied his request, a legal challenge followed. The FDNY maintained that under the state's Freedom of Information Law (FOIL), the oral histories fit into two exempt classifications: intra-agency communications and law enforcement records. The final court to hear this matter was not so persuaded. Instead, the Court of Appeals for the State of New York determined that neither of these exemptions applied: "We infer from the record that the oral histories were exactly what the name implies—spoken words recorded for the benefit of posterity—and that the Department intended, and the people interviewed for those oral histories understood or reasonably should have understood that the words spoken were destined for public disclosure."[24] In the end, the court did allow the FDNY to secure court approval to redact any material in the interviews that they believed could cause pain or embarrassment to an interviewee.

Only two states, Kentucky and Texas, have enacted specific legislation to exempt sealed or restricted interviews from FOIA requests. Although both enactments share a common purpose, the Kentucky statute specifically provides that "a state agency or institution which obtains an oral history interview for historical purposes may enter into a reasonable and mutually acceptable written agreement of confidentiality with the interviewee with regard thereto."[25] An oral history interview that is housed in a state agency in Kentucky that is not covered by a written agreement of confidentiality is considered public information and may be accessed by an FOIA request. The Texas statute is broader in scope than the Kentucky statute in terms of the archival material protected (oral history, personal papers, unpublished letters, etc.), but exempts such materials only if they were "...not created or maintained in the conduct of official business of a governmental body...." The Texas exemption also mandates that the materials, whether at a private or public repository, must be used for historical research.[26]

The statutory exemption in Texas is very similar to the protection offered to federal agencies that are statutorily authorized to accept and retain gifts, such as historical materials. An agency with such authority can in turn offer interviewees the opportunity to place restrictions on their interviews. To do so, however, the interview cannot come about because of a job-related requirement. For example, a required exit interview for a federal employee would not qualify. But if the same federal employee volunteered to be interviewed for an agency's history project, he or she could place restrictions on the resulting interview. These restrictions would preclude access via a freedom of information request.

The National Archives is also authorized by law to accept papers and interviews with restrictions. Since 1985, the Archives has encouraged federal agencies that are not statutorily authorized to accept and retain historical materials to utilize the Archives' exemption. To do so, the interviews must also be nonwork related. Employees who volunteer to be interviewed, however, can then place restrictions on their interviews, which the National Archives will honor once they are deposited. As noted by the National Archives, this policy recognizes "... that the quality of an oral interview can depend on the degree to which an interviewee is able to control access to his or her responses."[27] It should also be noted that the National Archives can also enforce restrictions that might be attached to historical materials (oral histories) donated by private individuals or groups.

CONCLUSION

For the vast majority of oral historians, subpoenas and FOIA requests may never come any closer to them than the discussion in this chapter. However, given the mind-boggling growth in volume of oral history interviewing with each passing year and the increasing emphasis by practitioners on more contemporary topics and issues, the possibility that more subpoenas will be served on oral history archives is becoming less remote. If this day does come, since there is no "archival" or "scholar's" privilege to stand behind, if disclosure cannot be avoided, then the final task should be to minimize the scope of the intrusion. Discovery statutes allow judges to quash a subpoena as overly burdensome or to issue a protective order limiting the scope of discovery. These conventional protective measures, if granted, however, would only serve to minimize the access. For FOIA requests, only Kentucky and Texas exempt oral histories, although many federal agencies, including the National Archives, can do so as well.

| 4 |

Defamation

On April 19, 1989, a sixteen-inch gun on the USS *Iowa* exploded during a training exercise. Forty-seven crew members were killed in this tragic accident. Intense media coverage followed. Charles Thompson II produced two programs for *60 Minutes* on the accident and its causation. He subsequently wrote *A Glimpse of Hell: The Explosion of the USS Iowa and Its Cover-Up*, published by W.W. Norton in 1999. The book was based in part on more than two hundred interviews. Daniel Meyer, an ensign on the *Iowa* at the time of the accident, was one of Thompson's most important interviewees. In 2001, four crew members joined together to sue the publisher, the author, and Daniel Meyer for defamation and false light. They maintained in their lawsuit that the book contained numerous falsehoods and suggested that their actions led directly to the death of forty-seven sailors on the *Iowa*. The lawsuit against the author and Meyer was eventually dismissed because the court determined they had insufficient contact with the state of South Carolina where the suit was filed.[1]

The case is instructive because it demonstrates the chain of liability that can arise in any defamation lawsuit that involves the publication of material drawn from interviews. Though the publisher and writer or producer are always the primary defendants in such lawsuits, if the words of an interviewee are part of the claimed defamation, then he or she will most likely be named as a defendant as well. The chain in this instance actually began with Meyer, who provided the interview material that Thomson elected to use in his book, which W. W. Norton in turn published.

Given the extensive coverage that the national media gives to high-profile defamation cases, the impression that most Americans seem to have is that this sort of lawsuit is something that only stars and celebrities have to worry about. In 2008, for example, baseball pitching great Roger Clemens was pursuing a lawsuit against Brian McNamee, his former trainer, regarding the latter's claim that he facilitated the pitcher's use of performance-enhancing drugs. But despite the media's focus on the rich and famous, lawsuits for defamation are filed every day in local courts across the country. One good indication of the frequency of such lawsuits is the annual fifty-state surveys (including Canada) that the Media Law Resource Center (MLRC), a nonprofit clearing house, has been publishing since the early 1980s. This three-volume report is put together by the MLRC to assist lawyers and interested parties in dealing with defamation lawsuits in their respective jurisdictions. A surprisingly large number of the individuals who file these lawsuits are neither celebrities nor public figures.

The manner in which an individual is portrayed to the general public is a branch of tort law. A tort is a civil wrong or injury other than a breach of contract. Defamation is the omnibus term that encompasses injury to one's reputation by libel, the written word, and/or slander, the spoken word. It is usually defined as "a false statement of fact printed or broadcast about a person which tends to injure that person's interest."[2] The readiness of individuals and organizations to go to court to protect their reputations is something that Samuel Johnson, the great eighteenth-century English writer and poet, recognized more than two centuries ago: "Defamation is sufficiently copious. The general lampooner of mankind may find long exercise for his zeal or wit, in the defects of nature, the vexations of life, the follies of opinion, and the corruptions of practice."[3] Unfortunately, lawsuits for defamation are certainly still quite copious today.

From a layperson's standpoint, defamation lawsuits often seem petty and rather confusing. This view is also shared by many in the legal profession. Even one of the great authorities on the subject, William Prosser, begins his attempt to explain this area of the law with the admission, "There is a great deal in the law of defamation which makes no sense."[4] What makes this area of law even more confusing is the coexistence of both state and federal law. The landmark decision in 1964 by the U.S. Supreme Court in *New York Times Co. v. Sullivan* recognized that free speech under the First Amendment could be severely abridged if lawsuits for defamation were not restricted in some way. The mechanism that they devised was to create a much higher burden of proof for people who were in the public eye. In this way, the Supreme Court sought to limit the number of lawsuits that individuals who were considered to be public figures would bring.[5]

REPUBLISHERS BEWARE

What concern is all this for oral historians? If an interviewee in a careless moment utters some words that later turn out to be defamatory, is that not the interviewee's problem? Yes, it is, but almost certainly it will also be the problem of the oral history program that made available to the public the recording or transcript containing the defamatory language. The rule as set out in the authoritative *Restatement (Second) of Torts* is: "...one who repeats or otherwise republishes defamatory matter is subject to the liability as if he had originally published it."[6] Stated in more colloquial terms, talebearers are as liable as talemakers. The applicability of this rule was clearly demonstrated in the case involving the USS *Iowa*. The interviewee, Daniel Meyer, was the original source of the alleged defamation; the author, Charles Thompson II, was the initial recipient of the material, and when he included it in his book he became a republisher along with W. W. Norton.

A 2005 case that directly involved a major oral history program, *Hebrew Academy of San Francisco v. Regents of University of California*, is worthy of extended discussion because it demonstrates how even limited distribution of the transcript of an interview is enough to establish the program as a republisher.[7] This lawsuit arose from interviews that the Regional Oral History Office (ROHO) of the University of California, Berkeley, conducted in 1992 for the Jewish Community Federation of San Francisco. The goal of the project was to document Jewish philanthropy in the San Francisco area by interviewing the fifteen past presidents of the federation. In 1992 a ROHO interviewer conducted four interviews with Richard N. Goldman, one of the past presidents. After he reviewed his interviews, a 102-page transcript was deposited in the Bancroft Library (Berkeley) and the Charles E. Young Research Library (UCLA). The copyrighted transcript was subsequently sent to four other research libraries and listed on several internet databases.

In 2001, a researcher who was preparing to write a historical account of the San Francisco Hebrew Academy and Rabbi Pinchas Lipner, its founder and dean, requested selected pages from the Goldman transcript. When she came across statements by Goldman that were critical of the rabbi and the Hebrew Academy, she passed them on to Lipner. In 2002, the rabbi and the Hebrew Academy filed a lawsuit for defamation and false light against Goldman and the Jewish Community Federation of San Francisco. Shortly thereafter, the Bancroft Library and the Regents of the University of California were added to the lawsuit. The addition of these codefendants was predicated on the publication by ROHO of the Goldman transcript (by distribution to four research libraries), which Lipner's attorneys claimed constituted republication of the defamatory statements. In California, as in other states, talebearers (those who publish or republish) can be as liable as talemakers (Goldman).

Rabbi Lipner and the Hebrew Academy alleged in their complaint that Goldman's statements regarding a 1974 capital fund drive for local Jewish organizations "have injured them in their occupation, tend directly to injure them in respect to their profession, trade or business...." The allegedly defamatory portions of the transcript read as follows:

> GOLDMAN: It is a disgrace. I think [Rabbi] Lipner is a person who doesn't deserve respect for the way he conducts his affairs.... I don't think he is an honorable man. Anyone who would take children from a school and use them to protest by sitting in at the Federation offices is someone who doesn't appeal to me. I remember a couple of occasions visiting the Hebrew Academy. When he would walk into the room, the children would stand at attention as if it were the Fuhrer walking in. To this day, I don't understand how he's gotten away with it. I don't object to Jewish education but what he has gotten away with is hard for me to understand or accept....
>
> The Hebrew Academy has done little for the community. The excessive financial support of the school was and continues to be a terrible drain on the community through the Federation.... I know that as Russian immigration flourished, he was soliciting them to attend the Academy and then prevailed on the Federation to pay for their education. I don't think those people knew one school from another, but he was the first to approach them....
>
> GLASER: Despite how manipulative you describe Rabbi Lipner is in grabbing on to Russian children...
>
> GOLDMAN: I have just watched him in action over the years and I have no respect for him....
>
> I think he is self-serving and an embarrassment. He was run out of other communities before he got here. We are too tolerant of him.
>
> GLASER: Oh, I didn't know that.
>
> GOLDMAN: I'm not sure but I think he had been in Cleveland before he came here. Somebody checked the record and found that community did not tolerate him.[8]

After several failed attempts to have this lawsuit dismissed, attorneys for the Regents and Bancroft Library were able to successfully invoke California's anti-SLAPP statute. SLAPP is an acronym for Strategic Lawsuits Against Public Participation. The purpose of this statute and similar state laws is to enable individuals, groups, or institutions who believe their freedom of expression is being chilled or stymied by a lawsuit to sue for relief. The dismissal of ROHO from the lawsuit was predicated on the court's determination that the recording and publishing of oral histories qualified as a statement in connection with the public interest. Despite this successful outcome for ROHO, the case against the other defendants, Richard Goldman and the Jewish Community Federation of San Francisco, was allowed to continue.

A republisher cannot escape liability by including with the offending material the name of the person who originally made the defamatory statement. Nor does the republisher get a free pass if he or she accompanies the republication with phrases like "it is alleged that" or "it is rumored." As the First Circuit Court of Appeals noted, if the republication rule did not exist, "it would otherwise be too easy for a writer or publisher to defame freely by repeating the defamation of others and defending it as an accurate report of what someone else had said."[9]

THE ELEMENTS OF DEFAMATION

For a plaintiff to establish a case for defamation, *the Restatement (Second) of Tort* requires:

   (a) a false and defamatory statement concerning another;
   (b) an unprivileged publication to a third party;
   (c) fault amounting at least to negligence on the part of the publisher;
   (d) either actionability of the statement irrespective of special harm or the existence of special harm caused by the publication.[10]

The first element, (a), needs no clarification but the phrase "concerning another" sometimes can be a problem if the defamatory material does not directly reference or clearly identify the person claiming damage to his or her reputation. The test for this is usually whether a reasonable reader, viewer, or listener would readily be able to identify who was being referred to. The second element, (b), is literally satisfied by sharing the defamatory words with another person. However, this low threshold is misleading, in that a very limited publication may be found to have a negligible impact on one's reputation when and if the time comes to determine monetary damages under the fourth element, (d). The third element, (c), provides that the minimum level of fault is simple negligence. But based on *New York Times Co. v. Sullivan*, a much higher level of fault, "actual malice," is almost always required when the person claiming damage to reputation is a public figure. The fourth element, (d), while suggesting the potential complexity of the damage issues should a case get that far, can best be understood as requiring some actual damage to one's reputation. For example, persons who are especially sensitive and take offense over a false statement that a more reasonable person would simply shrug off might not be able to establish the fourth element because the damage to their reputation was *de minimus*. The fourth element, (d), also takes into account situations in which the defamatory statements not only damaged the person's reputation but also led to being fired from one's job. All states have criminal as well as civil penalties for defamation. Criminal prosecution, however, is a rarity.

The Dead Cannot Be Defamed

Although defenses to a defamation lawsuit are raised during the course of litigation, in order to be defamed, an individual must be alive. No one can libel or slander a dead person.[11] This prohibition gives authors a completely free hand when it comes to propounding novel or even shocking historical interpretations. Claims that Elvis Presley was a pedophile and Abraham Lincoln was gay are just two recent examples of such interpretations. Although some legal scholars have advocated an end to this limitation, there is no indication that this will happen anytime soon.[12] This rule provides a measure of protection to most oral history programs because interviewees often are recounting events involving participants who have long since gone to their graves. There is one exception, however, to this general prohibition. If a person was alive when he or she was allegedly defamed and actually commenced a lawsuit, the death of that person while the case was pending would not automatically end the matter in most jurisdictions. A lawsuit for defamation brought by William Jewell, the first suspect in the bombing at the 1996 Olympics in Atlanta, is a good example of this rule. After he died on August 29, 2007, his heirs elected to continue the lawsuit against the *Atlanta Journal-Constitution* he had started in 1997.[13]

Statute of Limitations

All states have a statute of limitations or maximum periods of time for filing most types of lawsuits. For a defamation lawsuit, the range is usually one to two years. The purpose of such statutes of limitations is to ensure fairness by barring the filing lawsuits for which the reliability of the evidence has been greatly diminished due to the passage of time. There are, however, exceptions to these filing limits, and this was the central issue in *Hebrew Academy of San Francisco v. Goldman* after ROHO was dismissed from the lawsuit. At issue was whether or not the so-called single-publication rule should be applicable to Richard Goldman's interview transcript. This rule basically holds that the initial publication of a book, newspaper, or magazine will be treated as a single publication for the purposes of any lawsuit for defamation. The purpose of the rule is to shield publishers from having to defend against a multitude of lawsuits in different jurisdictions. Thus, for example, if a book receives nationwide distribution, the party who is allegedly defamed by the work could file suit in only one jurisdiction.[14]

The issue before the California Supreme Court was whether the single-publication rule should apply to an oral history transcript that in this instance was first published in 1993 when it was placed in two research libraries. Although the court recognized that it was very unlikely that the plaintiffs could have learned of the existence of the Goldman transcript, since it was accessible only at the Bancroft and Charles E. Young Libraries, it still, however, fell under the single-publication rule.[15] Thus, the one-year statute of limitations to file defamation lawsuits in California began to run in 1993, when Goldman's transcript was first placed in the two research libraries. Since Rabbi Lipner and the Hebrew Academy did not file their lawsuit for defamation until 2002, the court held that it was barred by the statute of limitations.

Because California is a hot spot for defamation lawsuits, this decision is certain to be quite influential should a similar case arise in another state. The holding is a very reassuring one for every library or program that makes recordings or transcripts available to researchers. Had the decision gone the other way, and the court had held that the very limited distribution of the Goldman transcript did not trigger the single-publication rule, then every repository of oral history recordings and transcripts in California would most likely have had to audit their collections for potentially defamatory statements. Fortunately, that will not be necessary.

ORGANIZATIONS ALSO HAVE REPUTATIONS

This aspect of defamation law is sometimes overlooked because the vast majority of lawsuits filed are brought by individuals. But a business entity, political group, or nonprofit organization may also sue for defamation. The damage caused by the alleged defamation must be to the organization's or corporation's reputation *per se* and not to its individual officers or representatives.[16] In a 1999 case, *Smith v. Cuban American National Foundation*, a professor's statement about the apparent connections between the foundation's political contributions via a political action committee to various congressmen and the receipt of government funds in return was the basis for a defamation lawsuit.[17] Wayne Smith, a professor at Johns Hopkins University, made this statement during an interview broadcast as part of a PBS documentary, *Campaign for Cuba*, which examined the anti-Castro movement within the Cuban-American community. The lawsuit alleged that Smith's statement implied that the foundation was involved in either corrupt or criminal conduct because of the way that it contributed money and in turn received government funds. The lawsuit was eventually dismissed after the court determined that there was "substantial truth" in Smith's statement. As the court explained, "a statement does not have to be perfectly accurate if the 'gist' or the 'sting' of the statement is true."[18]

Public Figures Bear a Heavier Burden

Whether the individual bringing suit is a public figure or just a private individual will also have an important bearing on the ultimate outcome of the case. The decision which initiated all of this was *New York Times Co. v. Sullivan*.[19] This case grew out of an advertisement in the *New York Times* entitled "Heed Their Rising Voices." The ad, which was paid for by sixty-four civil rights activists, claimed that public officials in Montgomery, Alabama, had acted unfairly and illegally in dealing with nonviolent black protesters. Lester B. Sullivan, the police commissioner of Montgomery at the time, was not mentioned by name in the advertisement, but he sued on the theory that the ad imputed to him illegal and unethical activities. The case came to the U.S. Supreme Court after the Alabama Supreme Court affirmed the trial court's decision in favor of Sullivan and the award of $500,000 in damages.

At issue before the high court was a classic confrontation of private and public rights. If public officials were allowed to utilize local defamation statutes and take their cases before friendly juries in their home state, the First Amendment guarantee of free speech and press would have a very hollow ring. To right the balance, the U.S. Supreme Court not only reversed the Alabama Supreme Court but also rewrote the law of defamation. Specifically, the high court held that even false statements about public officials are entitled to constitutional protection unless made with actual malice (i.e., knowledge of falsity or reckless disregard of whether the statements were true or false).

In 1974, the U.S. Supreme Court in *Gertz v. Robert Welch, Inc.* completed its restructuring of American defamation law by establishing simple negligence as the burden of proof for plaintiffs who were not public officials.[20] In this decision, the high court also expanded the public official doctrine to encompass anyone who takes part in a public matter or controversy. In doing so, the Supreme Court established a two-step analysis to determine if an individual is a public figure: (1) whether a public controversy exists; and (2) the nature and extent of the individual's participation in the controversy. In essence, the decisions in *Sullivan* and *Gertz* have carved out a limited constitutional privilege to defame a plaintiff as long as he or she is definable as a public figure.[21]

Negligence versus Actual Malice

Two cases decided by the supreme courts of California and Texas respectively underscore how important the public versus nonpublic figure distinction is in deciding liability. While neither of these cases directly involved oral history interviews, both arose out of historical incidents that drew prolonged media interest and widespread national attention. The first event was the assassination of Senator Robert F. Kennedy on June 6, 1968, and the second the raid by the Bureau of Alcohol, Tobacco, Firearms and Explosives (ATF) on the Branch Davidian compound on February 28, 1993.

The first case, *Khawar v. Globe International, Inc.*, began with a book entitled *The Senator Must Die: The Murder of Robert Kennedy*, published in 1988.[22] Robert Morrow, the author, claimed that the Iranian secret police (SAVAK) and the Mafia were behind the assassination and that Ali Ahmand, a young Pakistani, actually assassinated Kennedy. In 1989 the *Globe*, a weekly tabloid newspaper, ran a story on the book entitled "Former CIA Agent Claims: Iranians Killed Bobby Kennedy for the Mafia." The article was an uncritical summary of the book's central allegation. It also included an enlarged photograph from the book of a group of men standing near Kennedy. An arrow beside the photo identified Ahmand as the alleged assassin. Following the publication of the *Globe* article, the man with the arrow pointed at him was determined to be Khalid Iqbal Khawar, a farmer living in Bakersfield, California. Almost immediately, he and his family were subjected to acts of vandalism, intimidation, and death threats.

After Khawar filed suit for defamation and a jury awarded him $1.8 million, the *Globe* appealed, claiming that Khawar was not a private citizen but a limited-purpose public figure. According to the holding in *Gertz*, this type of public figure is one who ". . . voluntarily injects himself or is drawn into a particular controversy and thereby becomes a public figure for a limited range of issues."[23] When the California Supreme Court applied the facts of the case to this definition, it determined that while Khawar had indeed been drawn into this controversy, it was the book and subsequent newspaper article that did so.[24] Just because he happened to be in a group photo with Robert Kennedy the day of his assassination while he was working as a photojournalist was not enough to make him a limited-person public figure. Although he had been questioned by the police after the assassination, he was never a named suspect. In the end, because he was a private citizen, all that was required was simple negligence on the part of the *Globe*, and there was ample evidence of that. If the Supreme Court had agreed with the *Globe* that Khawar should be treated as a limited-person public figure, he would have had to show that the defendants acted with "actual malice," a much tougher task.

The second case, WFAA-TV, Inc. v. McLemore, did not arise from the reporting of a new interpretation of a long past event, but from the second-guessing that occurred almost immediately after the bloody raid on the Branch Davidian compound.[25] John McLemore was a television reporter for station WFTX in Waco, Texas. After the station received a tip that a raid on the Branch Davidians by the Bureau of Alcohol, Firearms, Tobacco and Explosives (AFT) was imminent, he went into the compound with a cameraman. Two days after the raid, which claimed the lives of seventy-six Davidians and four AFT agents, a local reporter told Ted Koppel on Nightline that some AFT agents believed that David Koresh, the Branch Davidian leader, had been tipped off about the raid by members of the media. To support their position, these agents alluded to the presence of local reporters inside the compound before the shooting began.

WFAA, a Dallas television station, followed up on this claim the next day. The station broadcast a video showing McLemore inside the Davidian compound and identified him by name as a reporter for KWTX, Waco. The initial story indicated that McLemore and two reporters from a local newspaper were the only media representatives at the site when the raid commenced. Later that same day, WFAA corrected its story to indicate that only McLemore and his cameraman were in the compound when the shooting began. McLemore subsequently filed suit, claiming that the story implied he had tipped off the Davidians in exchange for permission to be in the compound when the raid began. As in the Globe case, the crucial question was whether he was a private individual or a limited-purpose public figure. In deciding that he should not be accorded the negligence standard, the Texas Supreme Court concluded that ". . . by choosing to engage in activities that necessarily involved increased public exposure and media scrutiny, McLemore played more than a trivial or tangential role in the controversy and, thus, bore the risk of injury to his reputation."[26] As a result, he was not able to show that WFAA's story was created with "actual malice," and his case was dismissed.

LIMITED-PURPOSE PUBLIC FIGURES

All-purpose or general public figures are easy to spot. The media provides us with endless accounts of what they have done, are doing, or are thinking of doing. In addition, public officials on all levels are generally considered public figures whether they are elected or appointed. Such a list would generally include "candidates for elective office, public employees, police and other law-enforcement officers and officials, and public-school teachers and coaches."[27]

Limited-purpose public figures are much harder to spot. For example, publicity that is given to a heretofore private individual does not by itself turn this person into a limited-purpose public figure. The first question to ask is whether or not there was or is a public controversy. The second question goes to the extent to which the person at issue chose to participate in this public controversy. In other words, did he or she step forward and take a leadership role or seek media attention? Finally, do the alleged defamatory statements relate to his or her actual role in the underlying public controversy or not?[28]

In both of the previous cases, *Khawar* and *McLemore*, there was a public controversy and the published statements about each certainly addressed their roles. The final decisions in their respective cases turned on the second question: did they knowingly engage themselves in the public controversy? For Khawar the answer was no; his life as an obscure photojournalist was long past, and when he was identified as the alleged assassin in the photo, he was a private citizen and nothing more. By contrast, McLemore was a working journalist who was covering a breaking story. His situation was far different than Khawar's. It is no wonder, then, that the legal skirmishing over the private citizen versus public figure status of the plaintiff is a crucial part of many defamation lawsuits.

Once a Public Figure Always a Public Figure

Although the U.S. Supreme Court has not as yet ruled on this important issue, the Second, Sixth, and Seventh Circuit Courts of Appeal have affirmed the doctrine "once a public figure always a public figure." In *Street v. National Broadcasting Co.*, the plaintiff was Victoria Price, the state's chief witness in the infamous 1930s cases involving the Scottsboro Boys.[29] Nine black youth, ranging in age from twelve to twenty, were charged with raping Price and another white woman, Ruby Bates. Their trials before all-white juries in Alabama created a national furor and led the U.S. Supreme Court to overturn two guilty verdicts because of overt racial prejudice. Price's lawsuit grew out of *Judge Horton and the Scottsboro Boys*, a television dramatization of one of the most dramatic of the trials. The script for this docudrama was based primarily on one chapter in a book entitled *Scottsboro: A Tragedy of the American South* by Dan T. Carter. Carter's sources included the official court transcript of the trial, news reports, the findings that Judge Horton made to overturn the jury's verdict, and interviews with the judge and others. The plaintiff, Victoria Price, alleged in her complaint that the television dramatization of this 1933 trial portrayed her as a perjurer, a woman of loose morals, and a false accuser of the Scottsboro Boys.

For all intents and purposes, the outcome of the case essentially turned on the question of whether Price was still a public figure or had become a private individual due to the passage of time. At stake in this determination was whether NBC's fault was measured by a standard of "actual malice" or simple negligence. Since the latter degree of fault would have imposed a much lower burden of proof on the plaintiff, the attorneys for Price naturally sought to have this standard apply. In affirming the trial court's classification of Price as a public figure, the Sixth Circuit held that "once a person becomes a public figure in connection with the particular controversy, that person remains a public figure thereafter for purposes of later commentary or treatment of that controversy."[30] It also extended public-figure-doctrine protection to historians: "Our analytical view of the matter is based on the fact that the Supreme Court developed the public figure doctrine in order that the press might have sufficient breathing room to compose the first rough draft of history. It is no less important to allow the historian the same leeway when he writes his second or third draft."[31]

In a 1996 case, *Milsap v. Journal/Sentinel Inc.*, the Seventh Circuit Court of Appeals reaffirmed the position in *Street*: "The Circuits addressing the issue have indicated that an individual who was once a public figure with respect to a controversy remains a public figure for later commentary on that controversy."[32] According to one of the leading experts on defamation, it is theoretically possible for someone to regain private figure status with the passage of time, but in all of the cases decided thus far, the "public figure status is a door that swings only one way."[33]

PURE OPINION IS NOT DEFAMATORY, BUT

According to the *Restatement (Second) of Torts*, "A defamatory communication may consist of a statement in the form of an opinion, but a statement of this nature is actionable only if it implies the allegation of undisclosed facts as the basis for the opinion."[34] The reason that expressions of pure opinion cannot constitute defamation is that ideas without factual grounding cannot be false. They are just ideas. The problem, as pointed up by the U.S. Supreme Court in a 1990 case, *Milkovich v. Lorain Journal Co.*, is that a statement that on its face seems like an opinion may actually contain considerable factual information.[35] As a result, the Supreme Court refused to endorse a wholesale defamation exemption because something is labeled an opinion. Instead, courts are to examine the setting and context in which a statement was made to determine whether it brings something more than an unsupported idea to the table.

The case of *Levin v. McPhee* demonstrates how statements from oral history interviews passed the confusing test established by the Supreme Court in

Milkovich.[36] In 1994, Farrar, Straus & Giroux, Inc. published a book written by John McPhee entitled *The Ransom of Russian Art*. In this book, McPhee, a prolific author, examined the unique art-collecting efforts of Norton Dodge, a wealthy University of Maryland professor. During the 1950s, Professor Dodge began collecting dissident art in the Soviet Union. For the next thirty years, from Stalin to *glasnost*, he made frequent visits to the Soviet Union and managed to take out more than ten thousand pieces of anti-Soviet art. The painters and sculptors from whom he obtained these works were of necessity clandestine figures. Evgeny Rukhin, one of the leading dissident artists, frequently traveled with Dodge to help him contact other artists.

In 1974 Rukhin and the wife of another nonconforming artist perished in an apartment fire of suspicious origin. In his treatment of Rukhin's death, McPhee presents oral history accounts from five people who were closely acquainted with the artist. All of the interviewees suspected foul play, but only three made a direct accusation against the plaintiff, Ilya Levin. One interviewee opined that Levin set the fire at the urging of the KGB; a second interviewee simply branded him a murderer; and a third interviewee suggested that Levin was a coward for not trying to save Rukhin from the fire. These accusations prompted Levin to file suit against McPhee and his publisher for libel. Although he lost at trial, he appealed to the Court of Appeals for the Second Circuit.

The central issue on appeal was whether under New York law McPhee could be found guilty of libel for reporting differing interpretations of Evgeny Rukhin's mysterious death. The court noted that while McPhee did not make the statements, his use of the statements made by the interviewees made him as liable as if he had made the statements himself. As for these statements— accusing someone of cowardice, conspiring with the KGB, or committing murder by arson—all would certainly damage anyone's reputation. But although these statements were clearly libelous if proven to be untrue, the case did not turn on the issue of truth but on whether or not the offending statements contained underlying factual information or were just pure opinion. In the end, the court was satisfied that McPhee's book had provided enough warnings to the reader that these accusations were "nothing more than conjecture and rumor."[37] McPhee and his publisher were thus victorious but only after an expensive trial and appeal. Obviously, the opinion defense to a defamation claim, like most of the other defenses—truth, consent, privilege, statute of limitations, and fair comment or criticism—must be asserted during the course of the litigation. They are not stop signs that can be raised to automatically ward off a lawsuit. The best practice is still to do everything possible to prevent the filing of a lawsuit rather than having to convince a court to recognize one or more of these defenses and grant relief.

The Major Categories of Defamation

Words and accusations that may injure a person's reputation are usually classified in most states into five major categories: (1) committing a crime, (2) acting immorally or unethically, (3) associating with unsavory people or otherwise acting disgracefully or despicably, (4) demonstrating financial irresponsibility or unreliability, and (5) demonstrating professional incompetency.[38] Bruce Sanford, one of America's leading authorities on defamation, has compiled a list of terms and phrases that he believes have the potential to be considered defamatory and thus lead to a lawsuit. A sampling of his so-called red flag words appears in the table below. As readers should note, all of these words fit readily into one or more of the five general categories of defamation.

TABLE 4.1 Sanford's Red Flag Words

addict	gangster	plagiarist
adultery	gay	profiteering
alcoholic	graft	prostitute
atheist	herpes	rape/rapist
bankrupt	hit-man	scandalmonger
bigamist	hypocrite	scoundrel
blackmail	illegitimate	seducer
booze-hound	illicit relation	sham
bribery	incompetent	shyster
brothel	infidelity	slacker
cheats	informer	smuggler
child abuse	intimate	sneaky
con artist	Ku Klux Klan	sold out
coward	Mafia	spy
crook	mental illness	stool pigeon
deadbeat	mobster	suicide
defaulter	moral delinquency	swindle
double crosser	mouthpiece	thief
drug abuser	Nazi	unethical
drunkard	neo-Nazi	unprofessional
ex-convict	paramour	unsound mind
fraud	peeping Tom	vice den
gambling den	perjurer	villain

From Sanford, *Libel and Privacy*, Sec. 413, 132, 11–13.

Professional Competency: A Special Concern

The case of *Hebrew Academy of San Francisco v. Goldman* was all about the professional competency of both the head of the Hebrew Academy and the school itself. Whenever an interviewee accuses someone of immorality or criminal behavior, the defamation warning signs should go up fairly quickly. Negative accounts about one's job performance or professional competency may be less likely to set off a defamation alarm. For one thing such statements are not as "hot" or sensational as allegations of criminality or immorality and many interviewers are often intent on finding out why a particular company, organization, or individual failed, succeeded, or chose to leave the marketplace.

A case involving Vincent Bugliosi, the celebrated author of *Helter Skelter*, helps shed more light on how a defamation claim can arise when one's professionalism is called into question.[39] Both Bugliosi and Earle Partington served as defense attorneys in the sensational Palmyra Island murder trials. In 1974, Muff and Mac Graham sailed to Palymra, an uninhabited island in the Pacific Ocean. They were never heard from again. In 1981, after the bones of Muff Graham washed up on Palymra, Stephanie Stearns and Buck Walker, who had been on the island when the Grahams arrived, were indicted for their murders. Partington represented Walker, and his codefendant, Stearns, retained Bugliosi. After separate trials, Walker was convicted and Stearns was acquitted. Bugliosi subsequently wrote a book about the two trials entitled *And the Sea Will Tell*. In 1991, CBS produced a television docudrama about the trials that was based on his book. Partington subsequently took issue with the negative portrayal of his legal skills and filed suit for defamation and false light. The representations from both the book and docudrama that offended him were his alleged failure to discover vital evidence, his overly submissive attitude toward the trial judge, his decision not to introduce a potentially exculpatory diary, his failure to call a key witness, and finally, a statement by the actor portraying Bugliosi to the effect that Stephanie Stearns would be spending the rest of her life in prison if he had defended her the way Partington represented Walker. The lawsuit was eventually dismissed because the Ninth Circuit Court of Appeals determined that Bugliosi's negative views of Partington's legal skills were protected opinion under the First Amendment. As the court saw it, "Because the book outlines Bugliosi's own version of what took place, a reader would expect him to set forth his personal theories about the facts of the trials and the conduct of those involved in them."[40]

The professional abilities of a scholar or writer can also be called into question whenever a reviewer pens a critical review of a book. While this happens quite regularly and may at times even prompt an angry response from the author, it can also lead to a lawsuit for defamation.[41] In 1985, Mark Katz authored a book entitled *Custer in Photographs*. William Gladstone's review of the book was syndicated in a number of periodicals. His review was generally unfavorable. While praising Katz for being able to compile 155 photographs of George Armstrong Custer, Gladstone pointed out a number of major problems: "His captions and documentation leave much to be desired. There is virtually no analysis or text of the photographs themselves. The scholar cannot use the book with ease for there is no index, footnotes or bibliography. I found too many errors in what had been presented and too many questions unanswered."[42] In dismissing Katz's lawsuit, the court held that criticism of a person's work product does not entail an attack on the author himself, and this review was well within the range of permissible criticism.

Suggestions for Avoiding Defamation Lawsuits

Fortunately, there is only one published case, *Hebrew Academy of San Francisco v. Regents of the University of California*, in which an oral history program was forced to defend against a lawsuit for defamation based on the publication of an interview. The best way to ensure that oral history interviews do not generate a future lawsuit is to put into place a comprehensive prevention system. While no such system can be made absolutely fail-safe, careful attention to the following suggestions will greatly reduce the risks:

1. *Staff Training*: Everyone who has some role in the creation, processing, editing, and archiving or retrieval of interviews should be included. This should also be a continuous process in which potentially defamatory statements are discussed and reviewed whether they come from your own interviews or other sources.
2. *Checklists*: Creating a series of questions to assess potential defamation is a good way to facilitate staff training. The following queries provide such an analytical framework:
   A. Is the subject living or active (individual or organization)?
   B. Would a reader's opinion or estimation of the subject be changed after reading the statement?
   C. Is the negative opinion expressed just that or does it contain supporting facts or at least imply them?
   D. Do you have other evidence to prove the truth of the interviewee's statement?[43]
3. *Verify/Seal/Edit/Delete?* Not every shocking statement or characterization is defamatory.[44] You may in fact be able to corroborate the truth of a statement by consulting written sources and even other interviews. The historical record is not and should not be something that has been sanitized by its creators and keepers. If, however, you are unable to corroborate the statements in question then start your damage control by starting first with the least invasive procedure. Sealing the portions of the interview that might be defamatory for an appropriate time period would faithfully preserve the historical record.

Careful editing of the statements at issue could remove concerns about publishing potentially defamatory statements but without greatly distorting the record. The last, and least desirable option in terms of being faithful to the historical record, is deletion of the material. This approach is certainly a form of censorship that is anathema to academic freedom and should only be used as a last resort.

But what if, just if, you receive a letter one day from a lawyer who represents a person or entity who claims they were defamed by something that one of your interviewees said in an interview? Such a moment is not the time to go it alone. Immediate consultation with a knowledgeable local attorney is essential. The money that you spend in retaining an attorney at this stage may go a long way toward resolving this matter before any lawsuit is even filed. Remember, litigation is expensive and often results in bad publicity, so whatever you can in good conscience do to head off or quickly settle a lawsuit is generally the most favorable outcome.

| 5 |

Privacy Issues

The Stealth Torts

The use of "stealth" as the defining adjective is quite appropriate for the three privacy torts that could possibly result in the filing of a lawsuit against an oral history program. Since there is much more limited awareness of these types of legal challenges, it is easy to overlook them. Their relatively low profile is due in part to the relatively small number of case filings that are based on one or more of these privacy torts. As a result, they generally receive far less attention from the news media than do the far more common lawsuits for defamation.

The creation of a right to protect one's privacy from unwanted publicity and intrusion was first propounded in a law review article written by Louis Brandeis and Samuel B. Warren in 1890. Until they published their seminal article, "The Right to Privacy," tort law had traditionally protected one from only physical harm.[1] Because of the technological advances that were occurring in the late nineteenth century and the aggressive expansion of newspaper reporting, Brandeis and Warren believed that protection from emotional harm was needed as well.

Legal protection for a right to be left alone has indeed become a reality. Today, this right to protect one's privacy is divided among four different privacy torts: false light, public disclosure of private facts, right of publicity, and intrusion upon physical solitude. Each of these causes of action offers protection for a particular aspect of one's privacy. Since false light is the privacy tort that is most closely linked to defamation, it is the most visible of the four torts. It has also produced a number of published cases involving interview materials. The next two, public disclosure of private facts and the right of publicity, are less well known primarily because they deal with privacy interests that are considerably removed from defamation. That does not mean that oral historians should consider these two torts as beyond the boundaries of concern. The ever-widening net of oral history interviewing coupled with the increasing scholarly and media utilization of these interviews make it imperative that oral historians understand what each of these three privacy torts entails.

Intrusion upon physical solitude is the only privacy tort that oral historians should never have to worry about. Lawsuits involving this tort almost always involve the news media. Most cases stem from overly aggressive reporters and photographers (known as paparazzi), who follow or stalk a person in public, take unauthorized photographs, and even trespass on the property or possessions of an individual. This type of information-gathering is something that oral historians simply do not do.

False Light

As a rule, most lawsuits for defamation include a false light claim as well. Since both causes of action require proof that the offending party published false information, there is a natural tendency to file both claims together. The elements of this privacy tort as defined by the *Restatement (Second) of Torts* are "(a) the false light in which the other was placed would be highly offensive to a reasonable person, and (b) the actor had knowledge of or acted in reckless disregard as to the falsity of the publicized matter and the false light in which the other would be placed."[2] To successfully prove up a false light claim, a party must be able to prove that the matter was highly offensive to a reasonable person, that the information was published to a substantial number of people, and that the publisher did so with actual malice.[3]

False Light versus Defamation

Although a lawsuit for defamation usually contains a false light claim, the two causes of action diverge significantly. The first major difference involves the words or images at issue. In a false light cause of action, the offending words do not have to be false as they do for defamation. This crucial difference can best be demonstrated by a lawsuit that was triggered by *The Hurricane*, a 1999 movie. Denzel Washington played the role of Rubin "Hurricane" Carter, a talented boxer who was convicted of murder and spent many years in prison before his conviction was overturned. The first three minutes of the movie reenacted the 1965 middleweight title bout against Joey Giardello. In this opening scene, viewers see a clumsy white boxer (Giardello), who appears to be in danger of losing the fight to the more talented "Hurricane" Carter. At the end of the scene, however, an all-white panel of officials awards the decision to a bloodied Giardello, with fans protesting loudly in the background. The clear impression that the opening scene leaves is that Giardello only won the fight because of the color of his skin. After seeing the movie, Giardello filed a lawsuit against the filmmakers for false light. The suit alleged that by all contemporary and histori-cal accounts Giardello was actually the better fighter on the night in question, his victory was a convincing one, and the fans in attendance were generally supportive of the decision. The two parties eventually reached a settlement agreement.[4]

Although *The Hurricane* accurately presented the outcome of the Carter-Giardello fight, what it falsified was the manner in which Giardello gained the victory. By depicting him as the weaker fighter who won only because he was white, the movie created an image that he deemed offensive enough to warrant a lawsuit. The human interest that is wounded or shattered by a false light rep-resentation is not a person's reputation, but his or her emotional well-being. For example, in Giardello's case, the wound was about how the film tarnished and cheapened his victory, not about how it falsely claimed he failed to defend his title.

The second major difference is the requirement in false light cases that there be considerable publicity given to the offending image or message. Thus, a larger audience must be involved to support a false light claim than one for defamation. The third key difference goes to the burden of proof that the person claiming to be the victim of a false light publication must establish. As noted in the *Restatement*, actual malice must be established on the part of the publisher. As in defamation cases, this burden of proof imposes a far heavier burden on the person claiming this emotional injury.

Unfortunately, even an extended discussion of what a false light claim con-sists of still might not make this very murky tort more intelligible. The murkiness, of course, comes from its all too close association with defamation. Courts are often forced to decide whether a plaintiff who his unable to make his or her case for defamation should be allowed to prevail on their fall-back cause of action, false light. As one authority has noted, "This somewhat nebulous area is a kind of expansion zone for the law of defamation."[5] Fortunately, a number of states have simply refused to allow this legal expansion to take place. In Wisconsin, for example, state law bars the bringing of any claim for false light. Similarly, the highest appellate courts in Colorado, Massachusetts, Minnesota, North Carolina, South Carolina, and Texas have ruled that no cause of action for false light may be filed in their state courts. [6]

Common False Light Claims

Even though the privacy tort of false light is not a valid cause of action in some states and looked upon with disfavor in others, examining the major types of factual situations from which most false light lawsuits emerge is still important. The most common one by far is distortion, or embellishment of the facts. While such distortions usually tilt to the negative side as in the Giardello case, it could also come about from an attempt to make someone look too good. For example, a local newspaper decides to do a feature on a Vietnam War veteran. Although the man served creditably, the resulting story embellishes his record with accounts of heroism and valor worthy of John Wayne. Even though such embellishment might raise his reputation in the community, he could still have an action for false light. The injury here would be emotional; he did his duty but is embarrassed by the license that the paper took in trying to make him out to be a superhero.[7]

Perhaps this scenario is a bit far-fetched, but it is reminiscent of one of the two false light cases decided by the U.S. Supreme Court. In Cantrell v. Forest City Pub. Co., a human-interest article examined how a family was coping with the loss of their husband and father, five months after he tragically died along with forty-two others in the collapse of the Silver Bridge that had spanned the Ohio River at Pleasant Point, West Virginia. Although the reporter for The Plain Dealer did not actually interview Mrs. Cantrell, he wrote, "Margaret Cantrell will talk neither about what happened nor about how they are doing."[8] Other portions of the story stressed that the Cantrell family was living in abject poverty; the five children were wearing old, ill-fitting clothes; and their house was in an advanced state of deterioration. While conditions were certainly not good for the family, their lawsuit claimed that the story made them objects of pity and ridicule. The Supreme Court ultimately upheld the Cantrell family's false light claim.[9]

The second major category of false light claims is false associations. In these situations, whether article, photograph, or media presentation is involved, the alleged offense is the innuendo that can be drawn from being shown with or connected to unsavory individuals or criminal events. A case from Illinois provides a prime example of a false light claim based on such association. In 2003, Harper-Collins published a nonfiction account of Michael Corbitt's association with the Chicago mob entitled Double Deal: The Inside Story of Murder, Unbridled Corruption, and the Cop Who Was a Mobster. Corbett coauthored the book with Sam Giancana, the godson of the notorious Chicago mob boss Sam "Momo" Giacona. In the photo section of the book, the authors included a picture of Gayle Raveling, Corbett's ex-sister-in-law. The picture was taken in 1983 while she was still married to Corbett's brother. The photo shows her holding Corbett's son, Joey, at his christening while standing beside Sal Bastrone, his godfather. The caption below the photo identified Raveling as Corbett's sister-in-law, and Bastrone is identified elsewhere in the book as the Chicago mob's North Side boss. She subsequently filed a lawsuit for false light claiming her association with the Chicago mob was highly offensive and caused her emotional distress and pain. The Court, however, determined that the mere inclusion of her photograph was insufficient to support her claim and dismissed it.[10]

Docudramas and Photographs

While articles and books can and do give rise to false light claims, such claims also arise from the fictionalized embellishments in docudramas or the placement of a photo as in the *Raveling* case.[11] Since docudramas often involve the use of oral history interviews, the case of *Seale v. Gramercy Pictures* is worth closer examination. The lawsuit was prompted by a docudrama entitled *Panther*, which chronicled the rise of the Black Panther Party. Because Bobby Seale was one of the cofounders of the party, the actor playing him had a prominent role. According to Seale, two of the scenes in *Panther* distorted the historical record and thus cast him in a false light. The first distortion involved Seale's effort to combat police brutality in Oakland by having the Black Panthers openly carrying guns. In one of the scenes in *Panther*, the actor playing Seale is shown buying guns from an Asian dealer in a darkened room. Seale maintained that the dialogue between the two, as well as the way the scene was shot, suggested that the guns he purchased to arm the Black Panthers were obtained illegally.

The actual fact of the matter was that while Seale had personally purchased the weapons to arm the Panthers, he did so in broad daylight at a sporting goods store. In another scene Seale and the actor playing Eldridge Cleaver are shown arguing about the role that violence should play in the Black Panther movement. Seale also contended that this scene cast his position in a false light by suggesting that he was an advocate of nonviolence rather than the self-defense position he actually had advocated against the police. In the end, the court dismissed his lawsuit because it deemed the distortions to be only minor deviations from the historical record. Even if the distortions had been found to be significant ones, the court opined that he was still unable to show that Gramercy Pictures had produced the scenes with "actual malice."[12]

Possible Links to Oral History

From the analysis thus far, the possible link that this privacy tort might have to oral historians appears to be very far removed at best. The cases discussed have involved a Hollywood film, a tell-all crime book, and a docudrama. The first two of these are not likely to be produced by oral historians. There is, however, no question that the publication and broadcast of oral history materials is on the rise.

One indicator of this is the inclusion of a regular media review section in *The Oral History Review* beginning in 2000. Today, almost every issue contains several such reviews. The subject matter of these media productions is also important to consider. Although documentaries that address noncontroversial subject matter continue to be the rule, a number of recent media productions are taking on topics like desegregation and integration, police brutality, and AIDS. While it is certainly true that a false light claim could arise from the manner in which a community's history was presented, documentaries that address cutting-edge issues and topics are much more likely to ruffle more than just feathers.

The second area where vigilance is required is in the use of photographs to illustrate a book of interviews. Proper captioning and placement are very important. All layouts should be reviewed to make sure there are no unfavorable innuendos that might be drawn from the placement of photographs.

PUBLIC DISCLOSURE OF PRIVATE FACTS

According to the *Restatement (Second) of Torts*, this cause of action applies when: "One who gives publicity to a matter concerning the private life of another is subject to liability to the other for invasion of privacy, if the matter publicized is of a kind that: (a) would be highly offensive to a reasonable person, and (b) is not of legitimate concern to the public."[13]

This definition can be better grasped if broken down further into the four elements that must be proven to secure any monetary damages:

1. embarrassing private facts must be disclosed;
2. the facts must be disclosed to the public in general;
3. the facts must be highly offensive to a reasonable person;
4. the facts must relate to matters that are not of legitimate public concern.[14]

This tort essentially allows recovery for truthful disclosures of private or intimate facts about a person that are not newsworthy. In other words, the private facts disclosed do not further public understanding of any newsworthy issue or incident whether it be contemporaneous or from the past. Courts also tend to customize the "highly offensive to a reasonable person" element to the local community or area and the offended party's standing in it. If, however, the information disclosed comes from public records (civil, criminal, or military), then the information is usually considered *per se* to be of public interest.

An Illinois case, *Haynes v. Alfred A. Knopf, Inc.*, effectively demonstrates how private facts can lead to such a lawsuit.[15] In 1991 Knopf published *The Promised*

Land: The Great Black Migration and How It Changed America by Nicholas Lemann. Most of his research for this best-selling work came from in-depth interviews with Southern blacks who had migrated to Northern cities from 1940 to 1970. The story of Ruby Lee Daniels is the centerpiece of the book. In telling her story, Lemann included some very private details about her sexual relationship with her first husband, Luther Haynes. After reading these details and other claims by Daniels that Luther lost numerous jobs as a result of his alcohol abuse and was a poor father, Haynes and his wife filed suit for defamation and public disclosure of private facts. As the court noted, the latter and not the former was the major claim in this lawsuit. One of the passages in the book that was the basis for the claim of public disclosure of private facts read:

> It got to the point where [Luther] would go out on Friday evenings after picking up his paycheck and Ruby would hope he wouldn't come home, because she knew he would be drunk. On Friday evenings when he did come home—over the years Ruby developed a devastating imitation of Luther and could re-create the scene quite vividly— he would walk into the apartment, put on a record and turn up the volume, and saunter into their bedroom, a bottle in one hand and a cigarette in the other, in the mood for love. On one such night, Ruby's last child, Kevin, was conceived. Kevin always had something wrong with him—he was very moody, he was scrawny, and he had a severe speech impediment. Ruby was never able to find out exactly what the problem was, but she blamed it on Luther; all that alcohol must have gotten into his sperm, she said.[16]

Luther and his second wife maintained that this passage and several others revealed his private sex life in embarrassing detail and "ridiculed" his lovemaking ability. In upholding the trial court's dismissal of their claim for public disclosure of private facts, the Seventh Circuit Court of Appeals held that the so-called private details were too general to support the tort: "No sexual act is described in the book. No intimate details are revealed. Entering one's bedroom with a bottle in one hand and a cigarette in the other is not foreplay."[17]

This case is instructive for a number of reasons. The plaintiffs, Luther Haynes and his wife Dorothy, could certainly be characterized as average Americans. At the time this lawsuit was filed, Luther was a homeowner and had worked for years as a parking lot attendant. Their decision to take legal action against the publisher and author of *The Promised Land* suggests that public figures are not the only ones who take offense and seek legal redress. The second lesson comes from both the topic and the historical approach. By focusing on a handful of migrants from Clarksdale, Mississippi, Lemann was able to more effectively dramatize the personal struggles involved in this monumental migration and resettlement in the north. Oral history was the vehicle with which he vividly portrayed this historical struggle, as it so often is in the telling of many social sagas. But in sorting through the richness of the detail, oral historians and writers still need to recognize that for some people, like the Hayneses, certain details may be offensive enough to sue over.

Disclosure of Private Facts in Public Records

A case in Idaho, *Uranga v. Federated Publications, Inc.*, demonstrates that even extremely embarrassing private details from years past may be disclosed if they were gleaned from a public record. In 1995, *The Idaho Statesman* published a front-page story recounting a 1950s controversy involving the homosexual solicitation of teens at the local YMCA. The "Boys of Boise" scandal, as it was called, resulted in a lengthy investigation. One of the boys who were implicated was subsequently kicked out of West Point. The retrospective newspaper article published the one-page statement he had given to police at the time of the original investigation. In this statement, he admitted having a homosexual affair with Fred Uranga, his cousin and classmate. After the paper refused to publish a retraction, Uranga sued the newspaper for false light and public disclosure of private facts. Since there was no falsity associated with the publication of the statement, the first claim was quickly dismissed. What the Supreme Court of Idaho struggled with was the question of whether after forty years his past conduct and name were still newsworthy. Because this information appeared in a public record, the court ultimately held it was still a matter of public interest and thus rejected his claim with a parting quote from James Madison: "Some degree of abuse is inseparable from the proper use of everything; and in no instance is this more true than in that of the press."[18]

Passage of Time and Public Figures

An older case, *Perry v. Columbia Broadcasting System, Inc.*, directly addressed this issue.[19] In 1968, CBS developed and broadcast a seven-part series on the history and culture of blacks in America entitled *Of Black America*. In the first program, "Black History: Lost, Stolen, or Strayed," Negro stereotypes in the movies were addressed. Bill Cosby, the narrator, prefaced the film clips that were presented by stating, "The black male was consistently shown as a nobody, nothing. He had no qualities that could be admired by any man or more particularly, by any woman."[20] Several of the film clips shown were of Lincoln Theodore Perry, a popular Negro actor from the 1930s, whose stage name was Stepin Fetchit. Cosby commented directly on how important Perry's movie roles were in creating this stereotype: "The tradition of the lazy, stupid, crap-shooting, chicken-stealing idiot was popularized by an actor named Lincoln Theodore Monroe Andrew Perry. The cat made two million dollars in five years in the middle thirties . . . It's too bad he was as good at it as he was."[21]

In dismissing Perry's claim for public disclosure of private facts, the Seventh Circuit Court of Appeals held that Cosby's commentary addressed his public life, and "the subject with which the film dealt, the stereotype, and erroneous characterization of Negroes in film was a matter of public interest."[22] The court also brushed aside his claim that almost thirty years had passed since he made his last film and he should thus be considered a private citizen by noting that he continued to perform, albeit in local clubs and on the radio. The consensus among courts is that the mere passage of time does not significantly erode the newsworthiness of an event or individual or the right of the public to know.[23]

Possible Links to Oral History

The possibility that personal details provided by an oral history interviewee could lead to a lawsuit for public disclosure of public facts is not that remote. Though there have been no published cases to date that actually document this situation, an experience provided by Valerie Yow, a nationally recognized expert on oral history, is very instructive. Yow conducted oral history interviews for the history of a psychiatric hospital that she was writing. One of her interviewees told her about the lengths to which a fellow psychiatrist went in their personal rivalry. The two apparently had adjoining parking slots. The interviewee described how the other psychiatrist had driven sharp spikes into the ground on the edge of his spot so that his rival would blow a tire if he ever crossed the line while parking his car. In the end, she left this anecdote out of her history of the institution because she feared that "this could have been interpreted as invasion of privacy because the incident reveals a personal, ruinous obsession that few knew about."[24]

There are valuable lessons to be learned from Yow's experience. The anecdote she chose to leave out appeared to be a truthful statement for all intents and purposes. Had she chosen to, she most likely could have found other interviewees to corroborate the story that the psychiatrist had indeed placed spikes on the edge of his parking spot. But a lawsuit for public disclosure of private facts is never based on falsehoods. Embarrassing private facts are the issue. So when deciding whether to include highly personal details in a book, anthology of interviews, or media production, step back and think about whether publicizing this information would be highly offensive to this person in the situation or community in which he or she is located.

A 2007 case shows that even the most newsworthy events can still strike a sour note with family members and loved ones and spark a lawsuit. On May 11, 2004, Sgt. Kyle Brinlee, a member of the Oklahoma National Guard, was killed in Iraq. Because he was the first member of the Oklahoma National Guard to die in action since the Korean War, there was considerable media attention. A photograph of Brinlee lying in an open casket was subsequently published by *Harper's* magazine. The family was deeply offended and filed a lawsuit for public disclosure of private facts as well as intrusion upon solitude. In upholding the trial court's dismissal of the case, the Tenth Circuit Court of Appeals held that Sgt. Brinlee's funeral was unfortunately a very newsworthy event to which the public had been invited, and as such did not constitute public disclosure of private facts or intrusion upon the solitude of the family.[25]

RIGHT OF PUBLICITY

This is the third privacy tort that oral historians need to be able to recognize. Although it is far less likely to ever come into play in the shape of a lawsuit than false light or public disclosure of private facts, it still must be addressed. The right of publicity is something that each person has. This right allows us to prohibit someone from using our name, personality, or likeness for advertising purposes or commercial gain. It is defined by the *Restatement (Second) of Torts*: "One who appropriates to his own use or benefit the name or likeness of another is subject to liability to the other for invasion of privacy."[26] The right of publicity is first and foremost a property right and thus almost always involves the commercial use of someone's name or likeness, most often a celebrity or public figure. But this tort may also apply to noncommercial uses in which someone's likeness or name is used in a not-for-profit publication or broadcast. The privacy interest at issue is not financial gain but one's personal feelings, not wanting to be singled out or spotlighted. Awareness of this has prompted a few oral history programs to actually include a right of publicity clause in their legal release agreements such as: "I hereby authorize the use of my name, likeness and voice in the promotion of any noncommercial publication or broadcast."[27]

Two cases illustrate what manner and types of publication can prompt the filing of a right of publicity lawsuit. In *Tellado v. Time-Life Books, Inc.*, the publishers used a particularly harrowing photo of several American soldiers to promote a multi-volume series of illustrated books entitled *The Vietnam Experience*.[28] The photo had been taken immediately after a bloody "search and destroy" mission. The most prominent infantryman in the photo was Edward Tellado. In the photo, which was featured in brochures, mailings, and media clips, an anguished and dazed looking Tellado with rosary beads hanging from his neck was readily identifiable. He had discovered the photo while emptying a trash can in the course of his postwar job as a janitor. The caption below the photograph in the promotional letter he found read: "THE FACES OF BATTLE. U.S. infantrymen, some of them wounded, some dazed, and most of them frightened, await helicopter evacuation moments after a fierce fire fight."[29] Because he was still trying to escape from his war memories, finding out that his trauma was being used to promote the sale of books was very unsettling. He subsequently sued for false light and right of publicity. Although his false light claim was dismissed, the court held that Time-Life's newsworthy defense did not bar Tellado's right of publicity claim because he was not a public figure and the uses made of his likeness were predominantly commercial in nature.[30] After this ruling, a settlement was reached on his right of publicity claim.

In another use-of-ones-likeness-in-advertising case, *Lane v. Random House, Inc.*, the publication at issue was a newspaper ad for *Cased Closed*, a book by Gerald Posner that supported the findings of the Warren Commission regarding the assassination of President John F. Kennedy.[31] To heighten readership interest, the ad featured photographs of six of the most prominent authors who questioned the findings of the commission and who had offered various conspiracy theories instead. Beneath their photographs, Random House printed the caption, "Guilty of Misleading the American Public." Mark Lane, one of the authors who had authored the best-selling work, *Rush to Judgment*, claimed infringement upon his right of publicity because of the use of his photograph and name to promote Posner's book. In dismissing his claim, the federal district court found that Lane's frequent lectures and writings on the topic of the Kennedy assassination made him a newsworthy figure about whom the public had a right to know whatever the context.

Possible Links to Oral History

Although the prospect of a right of publicity claim being raised would appear extremely unlikely, nevertheless, a program or individual oral historian who wishes to promote a publication by featuring individual interviewees should always secure direct approval beforehand for such use. This recommendation would apply to both nonprofit and for-profit publications, but especially to the latter. Some programs routinely include in their legal release agreement a simple right of publicity clause. While the *Principles and Standards* of the Oral History Association does not directly address this issue, this omission seems predicated more on the relatively rare occurrence of situations like this rather than any sense that obtaining permission is an unnecessary ethical obligation.

DO THE DEAD HAVE A RIGHT TO PRIVACY?

The simple answer to this question is generally "no." A dead person cannot be embarrassed or emotionally harmed by any private facts or publicity that cast him

or her in a false light. If, however, a person was alive when the offending publication took place and then died, in some jurisdictions the deceased's heirs may be
able to file suit in his or her behalf. The right of publicity is the only privacy tort
that survives the death of the individual. Although not all jurisdictions permit
this, in the states where it is allowed, essentially the property right that a famous
person has in his or her likeness passes to the heirs. They in turn can determine
who may make use of this right of publicity and legally file suit against anyone
who does so in an unauthorized manner.[32]

Conclusion

Although far less common than lawsuits for defamation, false light, public disclosure of private facts, and right of publicity are three causes of action from which
oral historians are not immune. False light is almost always in a ride-along position
with defamation. But as noted, it can have a life of its own if one who publishes
either overly embellishes the facts or fails to recognize how the way in which the
material is organized creates a false light implication. The second privacy tort,
public disclosure of private facts, is certainly one that oral historians need to be
more aware of. The confusing thing about this privacy tort is that it is not about
truth *per se*, but very personal facts that are of no real public interest and thus are
just highly offensive. The last tort discussed, right of publicity, is probably the
least likely to be at issue but is certainly worthy of serious consideration whenever
the name or likeness of an interview is used to promote a publication or program.

| 6 |

Copyright

The top ten lists were first used by David Letterman in 1985 as a way to heighten viewer interest in his *Late Show*. Since that time, top ten lists have become a staple in American culture. They apparently satisfy a craving to rank virtually everything from actors to athletes. Not surprisingly, there are even top ten lists of the greatest copyright myths. Although there are at least a half dozen of such lists, a law firm that specializes in intellectual property law culled through five of these and produced a more condensed meta-list entitled "Four Most Mythical Copyright Myths."[1] This meta-list, which of course ranks the myths in terms of frequency, effectively introduces the common misunderstandings about copyright protection that could result in the unauthorized use of oral history interviews:

> **The fourth most mythical copyright myth**
> Tie: If I use only a small portion of a work, I don't need permission to use it. & If the work wasn't registered or didn't have a copyright notice, I don't need permission to use it....
> **The third most mythical copyright myth**
> If I'm not making money from the work, I don't need permission to use it....
> **The second most mythical copyright myth**
> If I found the work online, I don't need permission to use it....
> **The most mythical copyright myth!**
> If I give the original author credit/include the copyright notice, I don't need permission to use the work....

Readers should keep these meta-myths about copyright in mind to better understand how to set up and utilize the most effective protective practices and safeguards to combat these all too prevalent misconceptions.

COPYRIGHT IN NONFICTION WORKS

Copyright is a form of legal protection afforded a wide array of creative works.
It is a system of property much like the ownership of land. The owner of a copyright may sell, lease, divide, or bequeath his or her interest. The framers of the
U.S. Constitution chose the economic mechanism of limited monopoly as the best
means "to promote the progress of science and useful arts by securing for limited
times to authors and inventors the exclusive right to their respective writings and
discoveries."[2] Today, copyright in the United States is governed exclusively by
the Copyright Act of 1976 and the Digital Millennium Act of 1998. These two
statutes completely modernized the Copyright Act of 1909, which was enacted
well before the onset of many modern media forms.

Since oral history is usually considered nonfiction, an examination of the
ability to copyright such works in general is necessary before the status of oral
history can be addressed directly. Under the Copyright Act of 1976, "original
works of authorship fixed in any tangible medium of expression, now known or
later developed" may claim copyright protection.[3] Qualifying nonfiction works,
categorized by the act as "literary works," are defined as "books, periodicals, man-
uscripts, phonorecords, film, tapes, disks or cards in which they are embodied."[4]
The scope of copyright protection for works of nonfiction is limited, however,
because such works are built on facts. The basic presumption is that all facts are
in the public domain. Thus, writers who gather facts, even if they are previously
unknown or overlooked, cannot copyright their findings because discovery of a fact
is not an original work of authorship. The interpretation that writers attach to
their facts is also not copyrightable because this also becomes a fact that is in the
public domain as soon as it is created.[5] The bottom line is that creators of works of
nonfiction, like an interview, may claim copyright only in "(1) the author's original
narration and original expression of facts, ideas, theories, and research and (2)
the author's original selection, coordination, and arrangement of material."[6] This
is called "thin" copyright as opposed to the higher level of protection offered to
those who create works of fiction. But even this more limited protection requires
a showing that the selection and arrangement of the facts display some originality. In the 1991 case of *Feist Publications, Inc. v. Rural Telephone Services Company, Inc.*,
for example, the U.S. Supreme Court did not consider the mere assemblage of

names for a telephone directory worthy of copyright protection because there was insufficient originality in the expression.[7]

COPYRIGHT PROTECTION OF ORAL HISTORY: A CASE STUDY

Although the list is not a long one, there are a handful of reported cases dealing with the copyright infringement of oral history interviews. One in particular, *Maxtone-Graham v. Burtchaell*, deserves consideration here because it points up how interviews with no real commercial value may still spark a legal battle over copyright. In 1973 Katrina Maxtone-Graham published a book containing interviews with seventeen women entitled *Pregnant by Mistake*. In the book, women candidly discussed their experiences with abortion and unwanted pregnancy. The names of the interviewees were changed to assure their anonymity. The copyrights for the interviews were held by Maxtone-Graham. Some years later James Burtchaell, a professor of theology at the University of Notre Dame, decided to write a book opposing abortion. He sought permission from Maxtone-Graham to utilize extensive quotations from *Pregnant by Mistake*. Although permission was denied, he included direct quotations from the interviews in his book, *Rachel Weeping*. The intent of Burtchaell's book was to critique published accounts of women who discussed their experience with abortion. Maxtone-Graham subsequently sued Burtchaell for copyright infringement. At issue were seven thousand words (4.3 percent) of *Pregnant by Mistake* that he used without permission.

Ultimately, the Court of Appeals for the Second Circuit held that the usage by Burtchaell constituted fair use and dismissed the case against him. What is significant about this case is that it really was more about principle than money. Although most copyright cases involve large dollar amounts, here, Maxtone-Graham wanted to prevent the use of pro-choice materials in an anti-abortion book.[8]

USING NONFICTION TO CREATE FICTION

The limited copyright protection for nonfiction works even applies when someone uses such a work to create a fictionalized account of a historical incident or individual. John Robert Nash authored two books on John Dillinger, a colorful Depression-era bank robber. Unlike previous writers, Nash claimed that his research showed that Dillinger did not die in the FBI's raid on the Biograph Theater in Chicago on July 22, 1934. According to Nash, he had been tipped off to the raid and thus sent a small-time hood named Jimmy Lawrence to the theater in his place. He then capitalized upon his supposed death by changing his identity, forsaking his life of crime, and moving to the West Coast, where he died in 1979. In 1984, CBS broadcast an episode of the detective show *Simon & Simon*, drawing directly upon Nash's unique historical interpretation. This episode tracked John Dillinger to the West Coast and intimated that by changing his name and appearance, he had effectively escaped his criminal past until *Simon & Simon* discovered his true identity. Nash filed suit for copyright infringement, claiming that CBS had infringed upon his historical interpretation.

In dismissing his case, the Seventh Circuit Court of Appeals in *Nash v. CBS* underscored the crucial difference between the protection that a fiction writer receives as compared to a nonfiction writer like Nash: "The inventor of Sherlock Holmes controls that character's fate while the copyright lasts; the first person to conclude that Dillinger survived does not get dibs on history."[9] If CBS had actually utilized a large portion of Nash's actual words as well as his narrative arrangement of the facts, the Seventh Circuit might have ruled differently. Likewise, had Nash conveyed his startling interpretation in the form of a novel, CBS might well have been found to have infringed his copyright. But, since all that CBS did was borrow Nash's historical interpretation and some supporting facts from his book, this taking was considered to be fair use.

This chapter provides a primer on copyright for oral historians. The modest goal is to first explain and then relate to oral history the major concepts and doctrines contained in the Copyright Act of 1976 and the Digital Millenium Copyright Act of 1998. Key doctrines like fair use, joint works, and works-made-for-hire will be presented solely from the vantage point of the copyright holder. Since virtually all oral history programs and individual oral historians routinely obtain assignments of copyright from their interviewees, this perspective is quite natural.

OWNERSHIP

Copyright protection begins at the moment of creation. In a typical oral history interview situation, this would be when the interviewee stops talking into the microphone or video camera. At that point, the recording of the interview would be enough satisfy the threshold criteria of the statute, namely, "original works of authorship fixed in any tangible medium of expression."[10] The vast majority of oral historians and programs at some point secure the transfer of the interviewee's copyright interests by means of a legal release agreement. An increasing number of programs that rely on volunteers or independent contractors to conduct their interviews are also securing releases from interviewers. Such an assignment of rights is specifically mandated by the Copyright Act: "A transfer of copyright ownership, other than by operation of law, is not valid unless an instrument of conveyance, or a note or memorandum of the transfer is in writing and signed by the owner of the rights conveyed...."[11]

Like the statute-of-frauds provisions that govern certain types of contracts in every state, if you do not get it in writing, you haven't got it. The rule is absolutely clear. If you want to be sure that an interviewee or interviewer has assigned his or her copyright interests to you or your program, there must be a signed written agreement. Although there is no statutorily designated language that such an assignment must contain to be valid, the true intent of the parties must be discernable from the language used.[12] A simple declaration such as "I hereby transfer to the Oral History Program all right, title, and interest including copyright..." is more than sufficient.

Joint Works

Although neither the Copyright Act of 1976 nor a precedential court decision definitively establishes that interviewers have a copyright interest in interviews that they conduct, there is a considerable body of persuasive evidence that suggests that this is indeed the case. The seedbed for this position is found in joint works doctrine. Copyright law recognizes that there may be more than one author of a work. A joint work for purposes of copyright ownership is defined as "a work prepared by two or more authors with the intention that their contributions be merged into inseparable or interdependent parts of the unitary whole."[13] Most authorities are in agreement, however, that the doctrine of joint authorship is one of the more puzzling aspects of copyright law. The most common examples of works with two or more authors are books, musicals, and computer programs. Whether an oral history interview qualifies as a joint work is still not definitively established, but there is substantial evidence that it does.

To begin with, several experts support this conclusion. Paul Goldstein, a noted authority on copyright, reaches this result by means of a comparative analysis of letters and interviews. The key difference he sees between the two forms of expression is that "the questions and answers that make up an interview are more intimately connected than letters sent back and forth in correspondence."[14] William Patry, another recognized copyright expert, also lends support to this position. He contends that in a typical interview the manner in which questions are phrased, the responses that are elicited, and the follow-up questions would all qualify as creative elements for copyright purposes. Despite the apparent eligibility that interviewers have to claim copyright, Patry goes on to note that such rights in an interview "...occasionally pose troublesome factual issues because of the lack of express intent between the interviewer and interviewee with respect to joint or several authorship."[15]

The affirmative assessments offered by Goldstein and Patry that the questions posed by an interviewer are copyrightable were confirmed in a 2007 case, *Berman v. Johnson*.[16] The investor and promoter of an anti–animal rights documentary film, *Your Mommy Kills Animals*, sued the filmmaker for fraud, breach of contract, and copyright infringement. Richard Berman and Maura Flynn claimed to be joint authors with Chad Johnson, the filmmaker, for copyright purposes and sought appropriate monetary compensation. This film attacked the philosophy and tactics of PETA, People for the Ethical Treatment of Animals. Flynn conducted a number of interviews, portions of which were included in the film by Johnson. The questions used in the interviews were drafted by her. These interviews were an important part of Berman and Flynn's claim of joint authorship. Ultimately, a jury found that Flynn's interviewing was independently copyrightable. Since this decision comes from a federal trial court and not one of the thirteen circuit courts of appeals, it does not establish a precedent and thus is only instructive.

There is, however, a case decided by First Circuit Court of Appeals that extends copyright protection to questions. In *Rubin v. Boston Magazine, Co.*, Professor Isaac Michael Rubin was the creator of a set of scales consisting of twenty-six questions that were designed to help individuals determine the essential elements of a loving relationship.[17] In 1977, *Boston* magazine published Rubin's scale in a general interest article on why people fall in love. The questions appeared under the heading, "The Test of Love. How to Tell If It's Really Real." The Second Circuit Court of Appeals determined that the questions created by Rubin were original forms of expression that were copyrightable and also held that the wholesale appropriation of his scale was not fair use.

The most compelling confirmation to date that both the interviewee and the interviewer should be considered joint authors of an interview comes from the U.S. Copyright Office itself. This position is set out in the internal policy manual of the U.S. Copyright Office, *Compendium II*. Whenever an application is received for registration of an interview, staffers are to consider the following:

> A work consisting of an interview often contains copyrightable authorship by the person interviewed and the interviewer. Each owns the expression in the absence of an agreement to the contrary. In the event that only one of the two parties, the interviewer or interviewee, seeks to register an interview for copyright purposes, the staff is instructed to seek further clarification as to ownership before proceeding.[18]

To be sure, the vast majority of recorded interviews consist primarily of words spoken by interviewees in response to questions posed by interviewers. But courts have ruled repeatedly that the respective contributions made to a joint work need not be equal in terms of either quantity or quality.[19] The major litmus test appears to be the original intent of the parties. Did they intend from the onset to inseparably merge their efforts to create a unitary whole?[20] Keeping in mind the typical oral history interview, the answer would seem to be yes. The interviewer is certainly the catalyst who brings the parties together. He or she also usually dictates the topics to be addressed and the nature of the coverage by means of the questions that are asked. Also, decisions to explore additional areas are also usually made by the interviewer.

The purpose of this discussion is to underscore the importance of securing copyright assignments from all interviewers who are not regular employees. The consequences of unplanned joint authorship are not comforting. The Copyright Act of 1976 provides that joint authors of a copyrightable work have an undivided interest in the entire work.[21] Translated, this means that a joint author may unilaterally exercise any of the five rights of copyright (reproduction, distribution, preparation of derivative works, performance, and display). Thus, a joint author can publish the work or sign a licensing agreement to allow a third party to use the work. A joint author may also unilaterally transfer his or her interest to another party. When a joint author dies, his or her copyright interest does not pass to the other author but to his or her heirs. The only duty that joint authors owe to one another is to account for any profits gained from the copyright and to share such profits. Co-owners of copyrights clearly enjoy wide powers of exploitation without the consent of the other owner. The uncertainties surrounding such a strange ownership relationship are why most authors enter into written agreements before they begin a joint work.

There is, however, one benefit that oral historians can derive from an interview or transcript that is denominated a joint work. This comes about when a program is approached by an individual or group regarding the possible donation of recordings and/or transcripts. If there are no legal release agreements for the oral histories, most programs are reluctant to accept such gifts even if the proffered materials are of some importance. If the would-be donor was the interviewer or has a written assignment of copyright from the interviewer, then he or she would presumably be a joint author. At the very least, any assignment made by such a person would convey the right to use the oral histories as the program or collection deems appropriate. The only obligation to the interviewees or their heirs, if they ever showed up, would be to account for and share any profits derived from the utilization of the interviews. Since the vast majority of oral history interviews never produce any financial gain, the chances of this happening are very unlikely.

A sample deed of gift agreement for an interviewer as a joint author appears in Appendix 1 (No. 7).

Works-Made-for-Hire

If one assumes that an interviewer is a joint author, another important copyright ownership issue may arise, namely, his or her employment status. The Copyright Act recognizes that many copyrightable creations are not simply the work of independent authors and artists. Employees and independent contractors often create copyrightable works for others. The work-made-for-hire doctrine is the mechanism by which the act seeks to sort out the ownership rights of the various parties who may be involved in the creation of a copyrightable work. Understanding and correctly applying the work-made-for-hire doctrine is especially important to oral historians because programs and collections often rely on part-time or freelance interviewers.

The Copyright Act sets out two ways in which a work may be classified as a work-made-for-hire. The first simply requires that the work be prepared "by an employee within the scope of his or her employment."[22] The second method covers a specially ordered or commissioned work that falls into one of nine categories: "a collective work, as part of a motion picture or other audiovisual work, as a translation, as a supplementary work, as a compilation, as an instructional text, as a test, as answer material for a test, or as an atlas."[23] Works that fit into one of these nine categories still do not qualify as a work-made-for-hire unless the parties also have executed an express agreement to that effect. The copyright interest in a creation that is definable as a work-made-for-hire belongs to the employer or commissioning party.

Because Congress failed to define precisely just who is an employee for purposes of this ownership doctrine, it has been left to the U.S. Supreme Court to provide such a definition. In 1989 they tried to do so in CCNV v. Reid.[24] At issue was the copyright ownership of a sculpture depicting a homeless family that James Earl Reid had created for the Community for Creative Non-Violence. In an effort to try to resolve the uncertainty about who is an employee when the copyright interest in a work-made-for- hire is at issue, the high court adopted a test based on the authoritative Restatement of Agency to help other courts resolve this ticklish issue. Unfortunately, the definitions in this Restatement are so elusive that such guidance has served only to muddy the waters further.[25] Asking courts to apply the dozen factors in the Restatement can lead to very uncertain results. A decision from the very influential Court of Appeals for the Second Circuit, Aymes v. Bonnelli, however, suggests that two of twelve agency factors are usually determinative of employment status: whether the hiring entity pays the worker's social security taxes and provides employment benefits.[26] To be on the safe side, three other factors from the *Restatement* should also be applied: namely, the level of expertise that is required to complete the work and whether the hiring party has the right to control the manner and means of production and assign additional work or projects.[27] If affirmative answers can be given to all five of these factors, there is a very real likelihood that he or she is an employee.

Despite the confusion, oral historians and programs to which the copyright interest in interviews and transcripts is important have several fairly straightforward options. If we assume once again that an interviewer is a joint author with the interviewee, then the question becomes how an interviewer who is something other than a full-time employee can be asked to give up whatever copyright interest he or she may have. This question certainly applies to interviewers who may be variously characterized as part-time, independent contractors, or even volunteers. For those programs and employers who wish to make sure that all non-full-time interviewers convey whatever copyright interest they may have, there are two basic options:

1. Have every part-time, independent contractor, and volunteer interviewer sign a work-made-for-hire agreement before they begin interviewing. This type of agreement does not secure an assignment of copyright interest from the interviewer but clearly designates the hiring or recruiting party as the author from day one of the relationship. This type of agreement presumes that the interviews to be conducted fit into at least one of the nine categories of work that the Copyright Act of 1976 requires. The most likely fits for oral histories are: a collective work, audiovisual work, compilation, or supplementary work.[28] Unfortunately, there are no clear-cut guidelines that accurately forecast whether interviews conducted by a nonemployee interviewer fit into any of the nine categories. But assuming such interviews do, another benefit of a work-made-for-hire agreement is that because the hiring or recruiting party is designated the author, the automatic termination of an author's assignment after thirty-five years does not come into play.[29] This statutory privilege was inserted into the Copyright Act of 1976 to protect authors and their heirs from long-term economic loss due to unprofitable transfers or assignments of copyright.

2. Have every part-time, independent contractor, or volunteer interviewer sign an assignment of copyright agreement before they begin interviewing. This type of agreement, as the name implies, directly assigns whatever interest that a nonemployee interviewer might have in any interviews he or she conducts for the hiring/recruiting party. The right to terminate an assignment of copyright after thirty-five years with proper written notice applies to this type

of agreement.[30] Common sense would indicate that only the most monetarily valuable works would prompt an interviewer or his or her heirs to seek such a termination.

If there is any doubt about whether the interviews that a nonemployee interviewer is conducting can reasonably be classified as being part of a compilation, audiovisual, collective, or supplementary work, then do not use the first option. The second option provides the surest and safest approach.[31] A sample work-made-for-hire agreement (No. 12) and sample assignment of copyright agreements (Nos. 5 and 13) are in Appendix 1.

The Five Exclusive Rights of Copyright

The treatment of a copyright as a singular economic interest sometimes obscures the fact that an owner actually possesses five separate and divisible rights. Each of these rights may be individually licensed or assigned depending on the nature of the underlying copyrighted work. The five rights of copyright are:

1. to reproduce the copyrighted work in copies or phonorecords;
2. to prepare derivative works based upon the copyrighted work;
3. to distribute copies or phonorecords of the copyrighted work to the public by sale or other transfer of ownership, or by rental, lease, or lending;
4. in the case of literary, musical, dramatic, and choreographic works, pantomimes, and motion pictures and other audio visual works, to perform the copyrighted work publicly;
5. in the case of literary, musical, dramatic, and choreographic works, pantomimes, and pictorial, graphic, or sculptural works, including the individual images of motion picture or other audio visual works, to display the copyrighted work publicly....[32]

How the utilization of oral history interviews interfaces with these rights are worthy of some discussion. Right No. 1 comes into play every time a program or archive makes a copy of a recording or transcript and sends it to a researcher or places an interview on its Web site. The researcher who includes paraphrases and direct quotes from interviews in an article or book also comes under No. 1. The preparation of a play, documentary, or edited compilation of interviews falls under right No. 2. For example, *The Boys of New Jersey* by Tom Kindre is an edited compilation of interviews with World War II veterans collected by the Rutgers University Oral History Archives. As Kindre explains, "In working with the transcript excerpts,

I have edited out repetitive phrases, and have in some cases shifted material from one point to another to make a more cohesive narrative, but I have added nothing, so there are no words that were not spoken by the storytellers themselves."[33] Because Rutgers allowed him to utilize the copyrighted transcripts on its Web site, Kindre was able to create a compilation which he in turn copyrighted. The creative elements that he added were editing and organization. If a program or archive commissions a play based on interviews, the performance of this play would invoke right No. 4. Right No. 5 would be triggered whenever a museum uses either audio or video portions of interviews to highlight an exhibit or collection.

Length of Copyright Protection

This helpful chart provides an excellent overview of the length of copyright protection for works created under both the Copyright Acts of 1909 and 1976.[34] The length of copyright protection for joint works and works-made-for-hire can be even longer. A copyright term for a joint work with two or more authors, that is not a work-made-for-hire, is 70 years after the death of the last surviving author. Works-made-for-hire are accorded 90 years from the date of publication or 120 years from the date of creation, whichever is shorter.[35]

TABLE 6.1 Copyright Duration Chart

Date and Nature of Work	Copyright Term
Published before 1923	The work is in the public domain.
Published 1923–1963 and never renewed	The work is in the public domain.
Published 1923–1963 and timely renewed	95 years from the date of first publication
Published between 1964 and 1977	95 years from the date of publication (renewal term automatic)
Created but not published or registered before 1978	Single term of 120 years from creation for unpublished works made for hire, and unpublished or pseudonymous works
Created before 1978 and published 1978–2002	Copyright will expire January 1, 2048.
Created 1978 and later	Life of author + 70 years

Licenses and Transfers

The transfer of all or even a single right from the copyright holder to another is called an assignment of copyright. The transfer of the entire copyright is what almost always occurs when an interviewee or interviewer signs a legal release agreement. The oral historian or program that is the recipient of such an assignment, of course, becomes the copyright holder. If, for example, an author decides after publishing a book that the interviews he or she has conducted should be deposited somewhere for future scholarly use, he or she could assign these copyrights to an archive or program. The receiving entity might decide in turn to grant an exclusive license to the local PBS station to broadcast portions of the tapes (right no. 1). In doing so, the archive or program could still retain all of the other rights of copyright.

As noted in Chapter 2, a growing number of oral history programs are at the time of copyright transfer routinely extending a nonexclusive license to the interviewee. Such a license permits the interviewee to exercise all of the copyright owner's rights including publication and distribution. The term of such licenses is usually limited to the life of the interviewee and does not prevent the program or archive from granting exclusive or nonexclusive licenses to others to use the interview materials. A simple clause in a legal release agreement is all that is needed to share copyright in this manner with an interviewee; for example, "This gift does not preclude any use that I may wish to make of my interview, including publication, during my lifetime."

Fair Use of Interviews?

The ability of a copyright holder to control what uses if any are made of a work is not absolute. The most important limitation is the fair use privilege. This privilege represents a kind of socioeconomic balance between the right to control and benefit financially from the use of one's intellectual property and the personal and public benefits that come from being able to use works that are protected by copyright. Fair use is worthy of in-depth examination because of the copyright holder status that most oral historians and programs have. A well-informed understanding of what does and does not constitute fair use is essential to determining how to recognize potential infringement. The fair use privilege is characterized by the Copyright Act of 1976 as a limitation on the exclusive rights conferred by a valid copyright. It is intended to foster the utilization of copyrighted works for such vital public education functions as criticism, comment, news reporting, teaching, scholarship, and research. The act contains a four-part test that courts are to apply whenever the fair use doctrine is raised as a defense to alleged copyright infringement:

> The fair use of a copyrighted work...for purposes such as criticism, comment, news reporting, teaching, scholarship, or research,

is not an infringement of copyright. In determining whether the use made of a work in any particular case is a fair use the factors to be considered . . . include:

1. the purpose and character of the use, including whether such use is of a commercial nature or is for nonprofit educational purposes;
2. the nature of the copyrighted work;
3. the amount and substantiality of the portion used in relation to the copyrighted work as a whole; and
4. the effect of the use upon the potential market for, or value of, the copyrighted work.[36]

An acronym, PNAM, is the best way to keep track of these four factors. P stands for purpose; N is for the nature of the copyrighted work; A refers to the amount and substantiality of what is taken; and M is the market, or the economic impact on the copyrighted work.[37] Courts are not expected to give equal weight to each factor. The greatest weight is always given to M, the impact on the market. Thus, if an infringing work has a commercial purpose, or P, it will usually have a difficult time getting past M.

One other consideration that needs to be addressed is the added importance given by reviewing courts to the nature of the copyrighted work, N, if the work is unpublished. A line of cases beginning with the U.S. Supreme Court's 1985 decision in *Harper & Row Publishers, Inc. v. Nation Enterprises*, added considerable weight to N.[38] This case involved the unauthorized publication by the *Nation* magazine of a small excerpt from former President Gerald Ford's autobiography, *A Time to Heal*. The excerpt, which amounted to fewer than four hundred words, revealed Ford's explanation for his decision to pardon former President Richard Nixon. *Time* magazine had paid Harper & Row for the right to publish excerpts from Ford's memoir prior to its release. After the *Nation* scooped the most important story Ford had to tell, *Time* refused to pay the balance due on its contract. Although the M factor clearly favored Harper & Row because of *Time's* cancellation and the real possibility of diminished sales of *A Time to Heal*, the Supreme Court also placed special emphasis on the unpublished nature of the memoir. They went on to reject the *Nation's* fair use defense and awarded damages to Harper & Row.

The Supreme Court's decision effectively created a kind of double standard in terms of how the four fair use factors are applied. A greater degree of fair use may be permissible if the underlying work is published as opposed to unpublished. In subsequent decision, courts that have adhered to *Harper & Row* have reasoned that infringing upon a work that is unpublished may very well deprive the copyright holder of the opportunity to determine when to publish for optimum market value. An amendment was added to the Copyright Act in 1992 to try and limit the amount of emphasis that courts can place on the unpublished nature of a work when undertaking a fair use analysis. There is no clear indication, however, that this is having much impact. Since the vast majority of oral history interviews are generally unpublished, the extent of the fair use that can be made of them is more limited than for interviews that have been published.

A close examination of several cases may help shed some light on how courts apply the fair use factors to both unpublished works and works of nonfiction like oral history interviews. In a 2005 case, *Payne v. The Courier-Journal*, the publication of quotations from an unpublished children's book generated a lawsuit for copyright infringement.[39] Tom Payne, a former basketball star at the University of Kentucky, who was serving a prison sentence for sexual assault, was featured in an article that appeared in the *Louisville Courier-Journal*. During his incarceration, Payne had started writing children's books. The manuscript of a new book which he hoped to publish entitled *The Angel Mimi* had been sent to his mother. While interviewing family members about Payne for the *Courier-Journal*, the reporter was allowed to read the manuscript and subsequently included 157 words from it in the story about Payne. The family subsequently filed a lawsuit for copyright infringement. The case turned on whether or not the fair use privilege applied. In its analysis, the federal district court applied all four fair use factors to the facts of the case. The first one, purpose and character of the use (P), favored the *Courier-Journal*. The court noted that the quotes taken from Payne's book were used to elucidate the new path that his life was taking rather than to give readers a sneak preview of his new children's book. As such, the use was transformative and not duplicative.

The second factor (N), however, supported Payne's position primarily because his work was unpublished. The court, however, found that the third and fourth factors, the amount used and the market impact (A and M), supported the fair use claim of the *Courier-Journal*. The direct quotes used did not give away "the moral of the story" nor were they so extensive as to be considered substantial. Finally, the court did not believe that the 157 words would have any adverse impact on the future commercial value of *The Angel Mimi*. If anything, the sympathetic tone of the article might well aid in the future sales of the book when published.[40] In the end, the lawsuit was dismissed. It should be noted that the fictional nature of the unpublished work at issue here was very important in putting the N factor in Payne's column.

Two other cases involving unpublished works of nonfiction are much more akin to the types of infringement that oral history interviews might be subject to. In *Love v. Kwitny*, a 1989 decision, the unpublished work at issue was a paper about the 1953 coup in Iran. The paper also included autobiographical information about Kennett Love, the author, who had been in Teheran as a correspondent during the coup. In *Endless Enemies*, a book published in 1984, Jonathan Kwitny directly reprinted more than 50 percent of Love's paper. Although the author claimed to have Love's permission to use the material, the trial court held that the amount taken exceeded any license to use that may have been extended and ultimately decided the case by a fair use analysis. Kwitny maintained that since Love's paper helped establish his main thesis about the CIA's role in the coup, he felt compelled to quote more extensively to provide the "full flavor." On the court's score card, however, the unpublished status of the paper (N) favored Love, as did the percentage used (A). In this regard the court noted that the only portions of Love's paper that were not quoted were the nonautobiographical segments. In the eyes of the court, Kwitny's taking amounted to "nearly every vital organ" in the paper.[41] The last factor, the impact on the potential economic value of the paper (M), which the court deemed the most important, also went against Kwitny. A subsequent trial was held to establish the damages owed to Kennett Love.[42]

Jacobsen v. Deseret Book Co., like the *Love* case, involved an unpublished work. The major difference was that Dr. Gene Jacobsen's memoir, *Who Refused to Die*, was a personal remembrance of how he survived both the Bataan Death March and internment in Japanese work camps. Jacobsen originally compiled the memoir for his family. Over the years, he continued to add material and after each revision would give copies to family and friends. In 1997, the Deseret Book Company published the first of a five-volume set of novels entitled *Children of Promise*. The novels portrayed a Mormon family during World War II. The story of Wally Thomas, one of the sons, closely paralleled the experiences that Jacobsen related in *Who Refused to Die*. As a result, Jacobsen sued the publisher for copyright infringement. After losing at trial, he appealed. In its decision, the Court of Appeals for the Tenth Circuit noted that close paraphrasing of Jacobsen's memoir was very evident and in some places his words were directly copied:

Who Refused to Die at 130.

> The assignment to be avoided if at all possible, was the 'honey' detail that daily cleaned the Japanese toilets and carried the contents to the farm where it was spread on the plants. The work was bearable but the humiliation was almost too great.

Children of Promise, Vol. 2 at 186.

> Each morning Wally would receive a work assignment.... [W]orst of all was the 'honey' detail. The work was not terribly strenuous but the humiliation was almost more than he could stand. A work crew would carry the contents of the outhouses to the fields, and then would spread the human waste around the plants in the garden.[43]

In the end, the Tenth Circuit reversed the dismissal of Jacobsen's lawsuit and sent the case back for reconsideration. This action was based on the court's determination that the novels were noticeably similar to Jacobsen's memoir.

These three cases provide some helpful insights into how the fair use privilege interfaces with unpublished materials. The unpublished status of Payne's children's book, Love's paper, and Jacobsen's memoir gave all three plaintiffs a head start in the fair use analysis since this put the nature of the work factor (N), on their side of the ledger. But because the *Courier-Journal* transformed Payne's work by using direct quotes to emphasize his new outlook (P) and did not commercially damage the future market for his book (M), it won the fair use battle. Conversely, Jonathan Kwitny's direct reproduction of more than 50 percent of Love's paper in a book that was a commercial success (P) and that took the most vital parts of that paper (A), clearly damaged Love's opportunity to cash in on his unique autobiographical work (M). Finally, since the Tenth Circuit did not undertake a fair use analysis before sending the case back down, the decision of the district court, which originally ruled against Jacobsen, is still instructive. The court began its analysis by categorizing Jacobsen's copyright as the "thin" variety, which meant "...that more similarity is required because less protectable matter is at issue."[44] Based on its reading of Jacobsen's memoir and the *Children of Promise* series, the court concluded that Wally was a very complex character and was not simply Mr. Jacobsen and "...that Mr. Hughes copied some facts from Mr. Jacobsen's memoir but not significant original expression."[45]

Obviously the Tenth Circuit overturned the district court's decision but only to the extent that Jacobsen's case was worthy of a full trial on the merits. Although a settlement agreement was reached, had the second trial gone forward, the unpublished status of the memoir (N) would certainly have counted in Jacobsen's favor. Most likely, however, the transformative use of the memoir (P) and its nonfictional nature (N) would have favored Deseret. The deciding factors would ultimately have been the amount and similarity (A) of the material used in the novel and the perceived impact on Jacobsen's ability to commercially exploit his memoir (M). This comparative discussion would have been far more enlightening had the unpublished works been oral histories. Nevertheless, one benefit of this discussion is how it demonstrates the close analysis that courts undertake when determining whether or not the alleged infringement is actually fair use. Similar in-house analysis should also be undertaken whenever there is a reported copyright infringement before any further action is taken.

SUGGESTIONS FOR ANALYZING POTENTIAL INFRINGEMENT

Before undertaking any action to stop someone who you think may be infringing upon the copyrights to your interviews (including the drafting of a cease and desist letter), you should undertake a careful analysis of the alleged infringement. Begin by preparing a detailed list of the similarities between the interview and the other work. This should include all direct quotes, close paraphrases, factual references, and organizational similarities. Once this is done, step back and assess the extensiveness of the taking and its substantiality. Then, plug in the this fair use check list:

1. Is the interview published or unpublished? (N)
2. Does the usage transform the interview or merely present it in repackaged form? (P)
3. Is the use commercial or noncommercial in nature? (P & M)
4. Is the amount of the copying substantial or relatively small? (A)
5. Is proper attribution made to your program or archive? (A)
6. Is the interview material that is copied the heart and soul of the work or something far less? (A)
7. Would a court be able to reasonably determine that the use harmed the future economic prospects for the interview? (M)

Although the unpublished status of interviews will always be a plus for the copyright holder in a fair use analysis (N), whether the use is for commercial purposes, and thus hinders or preempts the market potential of the work (P and M), is the real heavyweight in any fair use analysis. On the other hand, if the use is transformative and nonprofit in nature (P), this will be an extremely hard fair use analysis to win unless there is wholesale copying (A).[46] Remember, works of nonfiction such as oral history interviews have only "thin" copyright. Thus, the path to proving infringement is a much steeper one and should not be undertaken unless the misuse is egregious. One final consideration is that the failure to secure permission to use or quote does not bar an alleged infringer from relying on the fair use privilege.

Pre-Lawsuit Responses to Possible Infringement

Like any legal issue that arises, the first step should almost always be to resolve the matter before either threatening to or actually filing a lawsuit. Litigation is expensive and time-consuming. This is especially true in the area of copyright law. Lawyers who are specialists in this area are almost always located in larger cities and are paid handsomely for their expertise in intellectual property law. So unless you are fortunate to have an experienced copyright lawyer or two handy, the best first response to an infringement that you believe is serious would be to draft a cease and desist letter.[47] This, most likely, would be the same first step that an experienced copyright attorney might counsel you to do as well. Such a letter might take the following form:

May 16, 2009
Mr. Arnold Smith
Publisher
The Literary Press
1234 Author Lane
New York, N.Y. 40000

Dear Mr. Smith,

We recently learned that you published a book entitled *Stories from the Camps: POW Authors* by Brendan Braun. In chapters three and four, the author published extensive quotes from an interview with Jeremy Borden which we hold in our archive. Before his death, Borden also transferred to us the copyrights to all of his fictional stories and novels. Brendan Braun never received our permission to quote from the Borden interview and reproduced the most poignant portions of Borden's interview, about 35 percent.

We hold the copyright to Mr. Borden's interview and believe that Brendan Braun and The Literary Press have infringed upon our interest. The purpose of this letter is to request that you immediately stop all sales and distribution of *Stories from the Camps: POW Authors* and contact us about reasonably compensating us for this unauthorized use.

Sincerely,
Jordan Blake
Archivist
The POWs Oral History Collection
5678 Memory Lane
Warbridge, WI 20000

Such a letter accomplishes a number of important things. It puts the alleged infringer on notice, sets forth the date that you discovered the possible infringement, establishes your copyright interest, gives the alleged infringer a chance to offer some acceptable reason for the publication, and sets the stage for possible settlement discussions. There is no need to threaten legal action in a cease and desist letter. The purpose is to try and initiate discussion and possible settlement and not to needlessly antagonize the other party.

To Sue or Not to Sue?

For the sake of discussion let us assume that your cease and desist letter has not had any effect on the alleged infringer. The infringers, of course, may be the author and his or her publisher, a corporation, or even a state or local government. Let us assume further that the copyright has not been registered at the U.S. Copyright Office. Now what? It is at this juncture that a lawyer with experience in copyright law has to enter the picture. Without the benefit of the lawyer's knowledge of copyright law and litigation, it is virtually impossible to make a truly informed decision about what should be done. Some of the issues that a lawyer would help you resolve are:

1. whether or not the lawyer should send a settlement proposal to the alleged infringer;
2. what the risks and benefits of a lawsuit are (if no settlement can be reached), including an assessment of the costs versus possible recovery of damages should the suit be successful;
3. whether the copyright in the work that you are trying to protect is registered or not.

Registration Status Is Crucial

Although it may seem strange to suggest that the last issue, registration, may be the deciding factor in any litigation decision, the following considerations may alter this position. To be sure, copyright protection begins at the moment a work is created. Thus, an oral history recording becomes protected expression as soon as an interview is completed. The same is true for an edited transcript. Moreover, the Berne Convention for the Protection of Literary and Artistic Works of 1989, an international agreement governing copyright, also took away the previous requirement that authors or holders were required to affix a copyright symbol, author name, and date to their works in order to secure protection. It is still, of course, a very good idea to affix such information and notice to any copyrighted work.

Copyright protection does not, however, equal enforcement. No one can file a copyright infringement lawsuit unless the work they are trying to protect is registered with the Copyright Office. This rule is an especially important one for oral historians, who only rarely see fit to register their recordings and/or transcripts. There are many reasons for this. Registration is not free; currently the cost is $45.00 for a standard paper submission and $35.00 for electronic filing. If the work is unpublished, only one copy need be submitted with the application, two if the work is published. Awareness that oral history interviews have only "thin" copyright may further dissuade some oral history programs from bothering to register. There are, however, significant litigation-related benefits to registering prior to any infringement. These advantages in effect make it far more possible for someone with limited resources, who nevertheless possesses a valuable copyright, to sue an infringer. The first benefit is the right to receive statutory damages. These are damages set by law and do not require proof of the actual damages suffered by the copyright holder. The amount awarded is predicated on whether the court finds the infringement was innocent or willful and can be as high as $150,000. The second major advantage is the possibility that you may be awarded attorney's fees by the court, especially if the infringement was done in bad faith.

Since cost is probably the single most important reason that most oral histories are never registered, one money-saving avenue worth considering is to register a group of interviews as a "collection." This can be done by submitting one copy of the interviews together with a single application fee if the "collection" has a single title and displays some common order.[48] An interview project such as "Italian Immigrants in Chicago" or "Inmates of Alcatraz" would seemingly qualify as a "collection" for registration purposes regardless of how many recordings or transcripts there were. Registration can also be done retroactively. Although published material must be registered within three months of the date of first publication, unpublished materials like most oral history interviews need only be registered before the date upon which the alleged infringement occurred.

SELECTIVE REGISTRATION

Even with the more limited protection that the Copyright Act gives nonfiction works like oral histories, if you still would like to be proactive in protecting against possible infringement, a policy of selective registration is advisable. The hard part, of course, comes in determining which interviews merit registration. Several criteria may be helpful in this regard. First, do you have any interviews that might involve "thick" copyright? Interviews with writers, artists, musicians, or composers who have published creative works may qualify for greater protection. This is especially true if portions of their interviews discuss their creative process. A second category of interviews that might warrant registration are ones that are particularly rich or unique. Asking a simple question like, are these interviews so special that someone might want to publish them for commercial gain is one way to try and determine which interviews to register.

THE ORPHAN INTERVIEW PROBLEM

"Orphan works" is the broad term that the U.S. Copyright Office uses to characterize a work that contains enough originality to be copyrightable but whose owner or creator cannot be found. Such a work could be a film, musical recording, or a photograph. It could also be an oral history interview for which there is no signed release. Whatever the medium of tangible expression involved, anyone who wishes to make use of such works without a license or assignment of copyright risks being sued. As one commentator has noted, "This problem renders untouchable a large swath of existing artistic, literary, and other works...."[49] The scope and severity of this problem recently prompted the Copyright Office to undertake a major study involving public hearings and comment.[50]

The American Historical Association (AHA) was one of the commentators. The AHA sought to emphasize how the orphan work problem "...extends into the archives, hampering the historian's ability to work with the raw materials of history." Their response in turn referenced Ronald Grele's account of how the Columbia Oral History Office had dealt with the orphan work problem while he was the director. According to Grele, they used the "good faith effort" test in deciding whether to allow researchers to have access to oral histories without releases. If a reasonable search had been made to locate the interviewee and his or her heirs, then the interviews could be used. But as Grele noted, "...twenty years ago this passed muster with the general counsel's office, I doubt that it would today."[51] He is certainly right about that.

The problem of orphan interviews is doubtless a large one. It would be a rare program or archive that does not have a shelf or two of interviews that fall into this category. They may have been donated by a small project that passed out of existence or by a researcher who published his or her study, or they may have been conducted by someone who mistakenly believed that legal releases were not needed. Whatever their origin, these "orphans" often contain valuable historical information that cannot be replicated. The legislation recommended by the Copyright Office's report would bar owners of orphan works from obtaining monetary damages for infringement if:

1. the user conducts a thorough search to try and locate the owner;
2. the user gives proper attribution to the owner of the work;
3. the use was noncommercial.

However, if the work was used for commercial purposes, a user fee would have to be paid to the owner.[52] Since there are no indications at this time that these recommendations will become law anytime soon, current holders of orphan interviews must decide whether to bar all access or allow limited use according to the tenets of fair use.

The No Access approach is the safest and, unfortunately, one that most programs and archives seem to have adopted. The Idaho State Historical Society, for example, lists more than five hundred interviews on its DNI list (do not include). Most of these "orphan" interviews were accepted by the society with the hope that some day they might be able to remedy the problem by securing releases from narrators or next of kin. But unless such a legal release is secured, all of the interviews on the DNI list "...cannot be released to the public."[53] Other libraries have sought to avoid the problem entirely by simply refusing to accept interviews without valid releases.

By comparison, the Limited Access approach is clearly the minority position. The archives at the University of Illinois at Springfield, for example, include a few interviews without releases on its list of Abstracts of Untranscribed Tapes. Such interviews are termed "Restricted," which means that while they may not be quoted from or published, the listener is free, however, to extract factual information.[54] The District of Columbia Public Library's statement on access to oral histories provides another example of how Limited Access to interviews without releases can be achieved. Because the public library has actively sought over the years to expand its archival collections for the District of Columbia, these collection efforts have brought in some "orphan" interviews. The library also candidly admits that at least one of its own oral history projects which relied on volunteer interviewers resulted in a number of interviews without signed releases. For both types of "orphans," the library advises interested researchers that it does not own the copyrights to these interviewers and, therefore, "reproduction of oral histories without a release is not permitted."[55]

As explained at the beginning of this chapter, "Copyright does not protect facts—whether scientific, historical, biographical, or news of the day."[56] Hence, if a researcher takes factual information from an "orphan" interview and uses it in a publication or production, this is not copyright infringement. Copyright infringement upon an "orphan" interview that is a work of nonfiction would in all likelihood entail either very extensive quotation or full reproduction. This should be the most important consideration for libraries and programs to keep in mind when they are trying to determine whether to let interested researchers have any access to their "orphan" interviews.

RESOURCES OF THE U.S. COPYRIGHT OFFICE

User friendly is the best term to describe the willingness of the U.S. Copyright Office to serve the general public. The relative simplicity that characterizes Form TX, the standard registration form for nonfiction works like oral histories, underscores this point. Although thousands of lawyers deal with the office each year, literally tens of thousands of nonlawyers also are in contact with it annually. The Copyright Office publishes over seventy-five circulars and factsheets The single most valuable of these is *Copyright Basics*. This is a very readable and concise guide to copyright law in general. Inquiries and requests for circulars and forms can be addressed to the Library of Congress, Copyright Office, 101 Independence Ave. S.E., Washington, D.C. 20559, but the easy way to contact them is via their Web site, www.copyright.gov/. This site offers a wealth of helpful information and is easy to navigate. All of the circulars, factsheets, and registration forms can be viewed or downloaded from this Web site. It also offers a wealth of information from the most "Frequently Asked Questions" to how to search the records of the Copyright Office. There is also a new procedure, eCO Online System, by which any individual or organizations can electronically register, record, and deposit a work. The procedure is website-portal based, has a lower filing fee ($35.00), offers faster processing, and online status tracking. The next best registration method in terms of processing time is Form CO, a fill-in form that can be completed on a personal computer and replaces Forms TX (literary works), PA (performing arts including motion pictures), and SR (sound recordings). Finally, the Copyright Office maintains a staff of information specialists to answer questions. While they cannot give legal advice, they are very knowledgeable and helpful regarding most aspects of copyright law, especially registration. For general copyright information you may contact them either via e-mail at their Web site (Ask a Copyright Question) or by telephone at (202) 707–5959. For preregistration information, the e-mail option noted above is available, as is a separate telephone number, (202) 707–3000.

COPYRIGHT AND THE FEDERAL GOVERNMENT

The federal government cannot claim copyright in works created by its employees. Although it is without question the largest single creator, collector, and consumer of information in the nation, the Copyright Act of 1976 specifically assigns to the public domain any work "prepared by an officer or employee of the United States government as part of that person's official duties."[57] Thus, all judicial decisions, administrative rulings, official documents, and everything published by the U.S. Printing Office enter the public domain when they are issued. State and local governments, however, are not barred from claiming copyright protection in works created by their employees.

   Like many seemingly straightforward legal tenets, the prohibition against the federal government claiming a copyright interest in a work is not absolute. There are several major exceptions that can and do affect oral historians. An agency of the federal government is allowed to hire an independent contractor to create a work and in turn hold the copyright to this work. A second exception arises from the issue of whether a work created by a federal official or employee was prepared in the course of his or her official duties. A mandatory debriefing, for example, would be the type of interview for which no copyright could be claimed. But if a veteran civil servant volunteered to participate in an oral history project, he or she could claim copyright in the resulting interview.[58] Federal agencies that are statutorily authorized to accept gifts, such as the personal papers of someone who worked at the agency, can also allow interviewees to place restrictions on their interviews. Such restrictions cannot be bypassed by freedom of information (FOIA) requests.[59]

For those federal agencies that are not legally authorized to accept personal papers and other gifts, U.S. *Code Annotated* 44, Sec. 2111 empowers the National Archives and Records Administration to accept for deposit historical materials from other federal agencies "subject to restrictions agreeable to the Archives for their use." In 1985, the National Archives established a procedure to allow oral historians working for federal agencies to offer potential interviewees the opportunity to obtain copyright protection and also to impose access restriction. Although both the federal agency that conducts the interview and the National Archives have some say in what form these restrictions may take, the key point is that such protection from freedom of information inquiries (FOIA) doubtless encourages many federal employees to be more candid and forthcoming.

COPYRIGHT PROTECTION ELSEWHERE IN THE WORLD

The sole focus of this chapter is on copyright law in the United States. Most other nations whether by signing the Berne Convention, the General Agreement on Tariffs and Trade (GATT), or bilateral treaties have agreed to give legal standing to the copyrights of foreign nationals. But how much legal standing they have varies greatly from country to country. There is also considerable variance among countries as to the essentials of copyright law. Canada, for example, unlike the United States, recognizes "moral rights," which allow an artist to protect his or her creative work from future alteration or distortion. This right to protect the artistic integrity of a work can be invoked even if the artist has legally transferred his or her copyright interest. Canada also allows works created by employees of the national government to receive copyright protection. It is important to recognize that a work that has been legally copyrighted in the United States may or may not receive the same level of protection in another country.[60]

How to Dispense with Copyright

Let us assume that you have just read this chapter and as you contemplate the complexities of copyright and the limited protection offered to interviews, you are asking yourself if it is worth bothering with. If your answer is no, there is a simple way to dispense with copyright altogether. The public domain is exactly what it sounds like, a vast repository of works that belong to everyone. It can best be likened to a gigantic library that anyone can visit and utilize without limitation. Any work that one finds there is beyond the reach of copyright law. Works come into the public domain in various ways. The two most common points of entry are the expiration of the term of a copyright and creation by the federal government. One can, however, choose to place an original work of authorship like an interview into the public domain. This can be done by a simple renunciation of copyright. Thus, instead of the standard assignment of copyright clause in a legal release agreement, the following could be inserted: "In making this gift I fully understand that my interview/s will not be copyrighted by me or the Oral History Program but will be immediately placed in the public domain. This decision is intended to provide maximum usage by future researchers."

Taking such a step is something that oral historians should seriously consider if they have no desire to police their copyright interests and wish to encourage the greatest utilization possible of the interviews that they have collected. One caveat should be mentioned, however; if a preexisting legal release agreement requires the continued maintenance of copyright, putting such interviews in the public domain would obviously constitute a breach of this promise.

| 7 |

Oral History on the Internet

$\mathcal{T}$he World Wide Web not only democratizes access to oral histories but also serves as a wonderful development opportunity for archivists and librarians to demonstrate to their institutions that they are expanding the visibility and availability of their collections. At the same time, ease of access and instant portability of materials raise the possibility of far greater misuse than traditional onsite research. There are three key legal issues that oral historians should carefully consider when making the decision to place interviews online. The first and most obvious is copyright. The second is defamation, and the third is whether interviewees and interviewers legally agreed to electronic publication. This latter issue goes hand in hand with specific ethical responsibilities to interviewees that the OHA's *Principles and Standards* clearly articulates. As the following discussion will show, the uniqueness of the information superhighway has forced some modifications in the way that the laws of copyright, defamation, and legal agreements are applied; overall, however, the same law that applies at ground level is readily applicable in cyberspace.

Legal Authority to Upload

As discussed in Chapter 2, legal release agreements should include future use clauses that do not needlessly limit the options of a program or archives. Though this can best be done both ethically and legally by specifically stating that electronic publication of interviews is an option, a good case can be made that very broad future use clauses like "for such scholarly or educational purposes as the program shall determine" are also legally sufficient for uploading interviews to the Internet. However, two of the Responsibilities to Interviewees (Nos. 2 and 9) in the *Principles and Standards* of the OHA specify that narrators should be informed of the potential for electronic distribution and new technologies. Thus, if you rely on a broadly worded future use clause that makes no mention of the Internet, ethical considerations should certainly prompt you to fully explain that publication of the interview on the World Wide Web is one possible use.

So what cause of action would interviewees who are not pleasantly surprised to learn that their interviews have been uploaded to your Web site for the entire world to hear, view, or read have if they wished to press their case? One cause of action might be for breach of agreement. Since there would most likely be no real monetary issue involved, pressing such an action would be more akin to a spite lawsuit. A second possible cause of action might be for invasion of personal privacy. This latter cause is directly addressed by one of the pioneer online archives, the Civil Rights in Mississippi Digital Archives at the University of Southern Mississippi. According to its privacy policy, "It is not our intent to invade or compromise the privacy of those individuals whose names or photographs appear in the documentation presented. We have included only materials that are part of our open collections, excluding any documents that are restricted by donors."[1]

The Digital Archives' Web site also features a standard letter of inquiry that is sent out to individuals to both alert them to the presence of the online archive and to seek their permission to upload relevant materials. While the major audience for this letter is clearly the creators of written records and photographs, it could easily be used to locate interviewees. If a letter of inquiry does turn up the creator of a record, a form for permission to display online is then sent out. This agreement gives the Digital Archives permission to "display digital reproductions from the_____Collection on the Internet for use by researchers."[2] It further specifies that all copyrights remain with the creator of the record. Such sensitivity to the privacy interest of those whose materials are displayed on the World Wide Web should enter into the deliberations of all programs and archives considering which materials and interviews should be electronically published.

COPYRIGHT AND THE INTERNET

Before addressing some of the new legal doctrines that the federal courts have developed to apply copyright law in cyberspace, it is important to review the

limits of copyright protection for works of nonfiction that are uploaded to the
Internet. Fair use applies equally to an interview transcript that is accessed on-site
or via the Internet. What is significantly different is the ease with which one can
become a publisher in cyberspace. Because the Internet allows virtually anyone
to post material on a Web site, and hence become a publisher, this has also "...
brought potential copyright disputes to the masses."[3] Since such "open access"
publication effectively removes any unpublished standing that an interview might
have, as noted in Chapter 6, the extra benefit that unpublished works (N) usually
receive in fair use determinations would also no longer be available.

A second consideration is the generally agreed upon noninfringing uses that
a person can make of nonfiction material on a Web site without express permission. The following actions would seem to qualify as fair use if done by individuals
for noncommercial purposes:

1. making a paper copy of an online interview;
2. downloading an interview to one's personal computer;
3. taking a very limited number of quotations from an online interview for educa-
    tional, scholarly, or journalistic purposes.

An important corollary to No. 3 is the greater degree of fair use that is given to
quotations that are used in publications that employ the material in a different way
than in the original work.[4] To be sure, fair use is an affirmative defense that must
be raised in court either on a motion for summary judgment or at trial, but given
the very narrow copyright protection that nonfiction works such as oral histories
receive, it would be best to view the uses noted in Nos. 1–3 above as givens.

The misuses that should be of major concern to programs and archives that
wish to protect their copyrights are far more wholesale and duplicative in nature
and may involve commercial gain. Practices that could lead to infringement go
by terms like framing and linking. The first of these practices, framing, generally
involves the importation of content from one Web site onto another. For example,
TotalNEWS, an Internet news service, framed news articles from media outlets
such as CNN and *USA Today*. The articles were placed within frames containing
advertising and promotions for TotalNEWS. The media outlets filed suit claiming
both copyright and trademark infringement. In the end, TotalNEWS agreed to
stop framing and was allowed to display text-only links to the media outlets.[5]

In the world of oral history, framing could hypothetically occur if someone
decided to create a national Web site on the civil rights movement and unilaterally framed relevant interviews from other online archives. Such wholesale downloading and framing would certainly constitute unauthorized reproduction and
distribution even if the Web site was nonprofit in nature. On this latter point, a
2000 case, *Los Angeles Times v. Free Republic*, is instructive. The central issue in this

case was whether the conservative-oriented Free Republic bulletin board could post verbatim copies of articles from the *Los Angeles Times* and *Washington Post* so that its readership could react and comment. Although Free Republic was a nonprofit, the *Times* and the *Post* both claimed copyright infringement. Since Free Republic claimed its uploading was fair use, the court conducted a very thorough analysis of all four fair use factors (PNAM). The court ultimately concluded that three of the four factors—purpose (P), amount (A), and monetary impact (M)—favored the *Los Angeles Times* and the *Washington Post*. Interestingly, the only factor that the court conceded to the Free Republic was the nature of the copyrighted articles (N).[6] This finding was predicated on their nonfiction status. But winning one fair use factor was not enough, and in the end the court issued a permanent injunction barring the Free Republic from uploading any articles.

Linking is one of the most user-friendly attributes of the Internet. The use of hypertext links allows users to quickly travel from one Web site to another. It can also serve as a vehicle for copyright infringement. The law is very unsettled, however, on the type of conduct necessary for direct or contributory infringement to occur. The actual creation of a hyperlink is not an infringement of copyright. Such a creation only rises to the level of infringement when the clear intent of the originator is to incur direct benefits or to knowingly encourage other users to infringe upon the linked Web site. A 1999 case, *Intellectual Reserve Inc. v. Utah Lighthouse Ministry, Inc.*, demonstrates how obvious and intentional the linking must be to qualify as infringement. The Intellectual Reserve filed suit to prevent the Utah Lighthouse from posting the former's *Church Handbook of Instruction* on its Web site. After the court ordered the Utah Lighthouse to remove its posting of the *Handbook*, the Intellectual Reserve sought to evade this order by adding three hyperlinks to its Web site. All three of the addresses provided contained the *Handbook*. The court determined that Utah Lighthouse's addition of these three hyperlinks was intended to induce, cause, or materially contribute to the infringing conduct of another. Such contributory infringement of copyright therefore justified another court order to remove the three hyperlinks.[7] This remote possibility that the creation of a hypertext link may lead to copyright infringement has still prompted one of the leaders in posting interviews online, the University of Alaska Fairbanks Oral History Program, to specifically ask visitors to its Project Jukebox Web site to "Not re-post or link this site or any parts of it to another program or listing without permission."[8]

DEFAMATION ONLINE

No single legal issue seems to invoke more anxiety among oral historians than defamation. The fear of being threatened with or actually sued for defamation because of something that an interviewee said is always present. Because interview access policies that require researchers to come on-site are seen by some oral historians as the best means of reducing their legal exposure, the idea of placing interviews online may seem too risky. The general consensus among legal scholars, however, is that chat rooms, bulletin boards, and blog sites are largely responsible for the increase in defamation lawsuits involving the Internet. Nevertheless, the odds that someone might discover defamatory statements in audio or transcript materials on a Web site are certainly far greater than if the only access is on-site.

The downside of expanding readership by means of electronic publication is well illustrated by a 2007 case that involved a wedding photographer and a disgruntled father of the bride. After viewing the proofs of her wedding photographs, the bride was so unhappy that her father created several Web sites on which he posted some of the proofs. He accompanied the proofs with disparaging captions that called into question the professional competency of the photographer. Obviously, the Internet provided the father with the easiest road to publicize his contempt for the photographer with the largest number of readers. Besides filing suit against the father for defamation and false light, the photographer also added a cause of action for copyright infringement because the contract provided that the copyrights for the wedding photos remained with him.[9]

One of the key issues that courts have had to wrestle with is how to apply the single publication rule to the Internet. As discussed in Chapter 4, the purpose of the single publication rule is to shield publishers from multiple lawsuits in different jurisdictions. The rule is triggered by the date upon which the initial publication occurs whether it is a newspaper, magazine, or a book. As the California Supreme Court determined in *Hebrew Academy*, the first day that an oral history transcript becomes available for research is the initial publication date. But Web sites, unlike more conventional print publications, can be altered, modified, or amended at any time. Thus, how should the single publication rule apply? Although most state courts have not directly ruled on this issue, a decision by the Court of Appeals of New York has proven very influential. In this case, a former employee sued the State of New York for publishing an investigative report containing criticism of his abilities as a manager. He filed the suit one year after the report was uploaded to the state's Web site. Lawyers for New York moved to dismiss his lawsuit for defamation because it was filed outside the one-year statute of limitations. Although no changes or additions were made to the text of the report itself, other modifications to the Web site were made after the initial posting. The court ultimately held that the onset of modern mass publication that originally prompted the single publication rule was readily applicable to the World Wide Web.[10] Thus, if an interview that is uploaded to a Web site were to trigger a defamatory claim, and if the interview was not edited or modified, a strong argument could be made that the single publication rule commenced to run on the date that the interview went online.

Protecting Copyright Online

Although a large of number of oral history programs have created Web sites that provide online catalogs and interview abstracts, these types of sites do not have to worry about protecting their materials in cyberspace for obvious reasons. There are, however, a growing number of programs that are placing at least some of their interviews on the Internet. One of the important issues that must be addressed before doing so is to determine the best practice for protecting interviews online from infringement, whether it is innocent or willful. While there is considerable variation in how oral history programs address this issue, the copyright practices that most online archives utilize fall into three major categories: Click-Wrap, Notice, and Free Access.

Click-Wrap Agreement Web Sites

The term "click-wrap" agreement is derived from what are called "shrink-wrap" agreements. Such an agreement is bound to the product by plastic wrap and comes into effect when the buyer opens the "shrink-wrap." A "click-wrap" agreement can be a dialog box or a pop-up that greets visitors to a Web site. It explains the terms and conditions of use, notes any fees, and requires visitors to supply some identifying information and click on the "accept" icon or button before they can access any materials on the Web site. Such agreements are generally enforceable when they offer the only avenue by which to access materials on a Web site and adequately inform the visitor of the terms and conditions of use. Such agreements are also known as end user license agreements or EULAs.[11] "Click- wrap" agreements are, of course, the online version of what some on-site researchers must agree to before gaining access to archival materials. The enforceability of such "click to accept" agreements was recently demonstrated in a case involving clip art. A trade association was held to have infringed upon the copyrights because it failed to honor the terms and conditions of the "click-wrap" agreement[12]

There is no question that any visitor to a Web site that relies on "click-wrap" access is immediately made aware that the site's creators are very serious about regulating how materials may be used. The terms and conditions for use that are set out certainly are intended to dispel any Web surfer's misplaced notion that the material is free for the taking. The Densho Digital Archive, for example, which offers a wealth of archival material and interviews on the Japanese-American experience, greets the visitor with an imposing two-page "Agreement & Application." The first paragraph clearly states that you are entering into a binding legal agreement with Densho. In doing so you agree not to copy, download, or transmit illegally any portion of the archive and further agree to indemnify Densho for any breach of this agreement or the unauthorized use of its contents.[13]

Two other oral history programs that rely on "click-wrap" agreements for access project a somewhat less legalistic image. The University of Alaska Fairbanks Oral History Program's Project Jukebox provides a one-page user's guide to its Web site, which asks visitors to accept four conditions:

1. Users must not use the material for commercial purposes. Short quotes and references are permitted for instructional and publication purposes.
2. Users must provide complete citations referencing speaker, interviewer, date, number, jukebox program, and Website with URL Address.
3. Users must not re-post or link the site or any parts of it to another program or listing without permission.
4. Users must follow the *Guidelines for Respecting Cultural Knowledge* and the *Principles and Standards* of the Oral History Association.[14]

This Web page also provides contact information for anyone seeking permission to use or publish the materials (beyond limited quotation).

The Regional Oral History Office (ROHO) at the University of California, Berkeley, begins its "click-wrap" with a definition of oral history. Visitors are told that interviews are primary source material and thus "...not intended to present the final, verified, or complete narrative of events."[15] One of the conditions for access to ROHO's oral history interviews, however, is the visitor's agreement not to quote for publication without the written permission of the director of the Bancroft Library. This limitation is far more stringent than the Project Jukebox provision that users may publish short quotations and references from the interviews as long as proper attribution is made to the interviewee and the program. The latter approach is clearly more in line with the fair use privilege.

Notice Only Web Sites

The oral history programs that use this approach do not require visitors to either identify themselves or formally accept any conditions for access. The copyright limitations are, however, prominently displayed. The Web site of the Rutgers

Oral History Archives, for example, contains 469 interviews primarily with graduates of the University who served in World War II, Korea, Vietnam, or the Cold War. It was one of the first oral history programs to place interviews online. The introductory Web page informs all visitors that copyright to all of the interviews on the site is held by the archives. At the beginning of each transcript, users are further informed that "Permission to quote from this transcript must be obtained from the Rutgers University Oral History Archives."[16] A similar but more user-friendly version of the "notice with access" approach can be found on the Web site of the New South Voices Collection at the University of North Carolina at Charlotte. Visitors to this site, which contains over six hundred interviews, are informed on the "Copyright" page that "the materials included in this web site are freely available for private study, scholarship or non-commercial research under the fair use provisions of the U.S. Copyright Law. . . ." Prior written permission, however, is needed for any uses that exceed fair use, including ". . . commercial or scholarly publication, broadcast, redistributing or mounting on another web site. . . ." which may in turn involve the payment of fees.[17] Finally, the Web site of the Maria Rogers Oral History Program (MROHP) of the Carnegie Branch Library for Local History hosts thirteen hundred interviews on life in Boulder County, Colorado. The "Copyright & Permissions" page informs the visitor that the copyrights to all interviews belong to the program. Users are free, however, to ". . . quote portions of the interviews, in papers, articles and other written, non-commercial projects unless otherwise noted."[18] Users are not free, however, to download and preserve the sound from the interviews and are instructed to contact the MROHP and the Carnegie Library for permission to do so or to order audio copies.

The Web sites of both the New South Voices Collection and the Maria Rogers Oral History Program provide visitors with reasonable explanations of what generally constitutes fair use. They do this by making reference to key portions of the fair use clause from the Copyright Act of 1976. Users are also clearly warned that commercial use of the interviews will require permission and may in the case of the New South Voices Collection also involve a licensing fee.

Free Access Web Sites

A few oral history programs have chosen to avoid any mention whatsoever of copyright ownership and in turn place no restrictions on the use of interviews. The Web site of the Bland County History Archives in Virginia, for example, features interviews conducted by students at Rocky Gap High School. They are organized by project such as "The Veteran's Project," which presents interviews with veterans from the county who served in Vietnam or the Persian Gulf Wars.[19] A visitor to this site will not find any reference to copyright use limitations. The same is true for the Bridgeport Working Voices from the 20th Century Web site created by the Bridgeport Public Library. This site presents oral histories "... of the people who worked in Bridgeport, Connecticut, over the past century. Every decade is represented."[20] Finally, the Shenandoah Valley Oral History Project Web site offers interviews with a very diverse spectrum of valley residents, including poultry workers, environmentalists, community activists, Latino immigrants, gays, and ex-offenders. Visitors to this Web site are informed that all of these interviews have been placed in the public domain. The only request that is made to researchers who actively use interviews from the Shenandoah Valley Web site is to "... please credit the interviewee, interviewer, and the Shenandoah Valley Oral History Project if you use all or part of any interviews in a manner other than your personal use."[21]

Conclusion

A very important consideration in choosing the best approach to protecting interviews online is to try and anticipate the motives of potential infringers. In other words, is the infringer more likely to be someone who believes in one or more of the meta-myths about copyright or someone who knowingly infringes for commercial gain? Even though nonfiction works receive the most limited copyright protection of all creative works, extensive or wholesale appropriation of an oral history interview by either a misinformed or calculated infringer would certainly not be fair use. The best protection against the former type of infringer is information. The information provided to Web site visitors about the authorized uses that they can make of interviews needs to be spelled out. It is not enough to just inform visitors that they can use the interviews within the accepted standards of fair use. The lengthy discussion in Chapter 6 on what fair use means suggests that such accepted standards are not readily known at all. A clear and concise explanation of what constitutes fair use can be readily crafted by referencing the language contained in the Copyright Act of 1976. The Jukebox Project provides a good example of how this can be done.

The central tenet of the privilege of fair use as set forth by the Copyright Act of 1976 is the right to make limited use of a copyrighted work "for purposes of criticism, comment, news reporting, ... scholarship, or research, ..."[22] This is intended, as the title of this section states, as a limitation on the exclusive rights of the copyright holder. However, the policy of some oral history Web sites is to specifically prohibit any quotation whatsoever without permission. Even if the process for receiving such permission is a relatively effortless one, such restrictions still represent an unfair limitation on fair use. Permission-to-quote limitations may also be out of step with the *Principles and Standards* of the Oral History Association. One of the designated Responsibilities for Sponsoring and Archival Institutions is to "...make known through a variety of means, including electronic modes of distribution, the existence of interviews open for research."[23] The latter phrase "open for research" would seem to be ill-served by online programs and archives that are overly protective of their interviews and thus artificially try to limit what most would agree is legitimate fair use.

| 8 |

Institutional Review Boards and Oral History

ORIGINS AND APPLICATIONS

The first Institutional Review Boards (IRBs) appeared on college campuses during the 1980s. They were created to review and monitor research involving human subjects. Ethical considerations such as respect for all persons and justice in the selection and treatment of human subjects were to be the paramount factors by which IRBs judged each research study. If appropriate consideration of these ethical issues was not built into a study, then it could not be allowed to go forward. The impetus for such oversight was a combination of outrage over the Nazi experiments on Holocaust victims and the United States' own tragic Tuskegee Syphilis Study as well as the recognition after World War II that biomedical research involving human subjects had become an integral part of modern science and needed to be monitored in order to prevent further victimization. The current regulations on human subject research are found in Chapter 45, Section 46 of the Code of Federal Regulations. They are commonly referred to as the Common Rule. Eighteen federal agencies, including the Departments of Education and Defense, subscribe to these regulations and require that institutions which receive federal funds for human subject research must create Institutional Review Boards to apply the Common Rule. Ironically, the National Endowment for the Humanities, which is the federal agency most likely to provide financial support for oral history research, is noticeably absent from this list.

Although institutions are not required to apply the Common Rule to research that is not funded in some way by these eighteen federal agencies, the vast majority of colleges and universities tend to err on the safe side and thus require their Institutional Review Boards to review all human subject research regardless of funding. This expanded oversight has proven particularly troublesome for researchers from the humanities and social sciences. Even when such researchers have no federal funding, they are still required to undergo an IRB review before they can begin their research. The biomedical orientation of most IRBs in turn often leads the board members to presume that qualitative research like oral history poses far more risks to human subjects than it actually does. This mind-set in turn often prevents IRBs from giving behavioral and social science researchers reasonable latitude to conduct their studies in accordance with the professional dictates of their respective disciplines. As noted by the Association for the Advancement of Human Research Protection Programs (AAHRPP), the leading national accreditation organization for human research protection programs, "The federal regulations are broad and subject to over-interpretation by risk-averse IRBs and universities."[1] As a result, most IRBs are unwilling to even explore the flexibility that the Common Rule allows for most behavioral and social science research.

Qualitative researchers in disciplines such as history, geography, and English on campuses across the nation are thus forced to seek approval from IRBs, which often require strict compliance to procedures that were designed to prevent abuse by biomedical researchers. Abnormally restrictive confidentially requirements, prior approval of questions for oral history interviews, absurd security provisions for recordings, and consent forms that inflate the dangers associated with being interviewed are only some of the many horror stories that have been recounted by researchers.

More recourse to legal action by frustrated researchers may well be just over the horizon. An attempt to help students better understand the culture of a historic New York City neighborhood led to an extended confrontation between the historian who developed the project and the IRB that demanded that it be reviewed and approved before any interviews were conducted. Rather than cave in to the IRB, the historian hired a lawyer to help her and after months of negotiation finally got the IRB to concede that her research was exempt.[2] Philip Hamburger, a law professor at Columbia University, contends that by applying the biomedically generated Common Rule to qualitative research, IRBs are constantly violating the First Amendment. He also argues that such application violates the equal protection clause because it selectively restricts the right of qualitative researchers to conduct and disseminate their research.[3]

As already noted, the heavy-handed treatment that most IRBs give to behavioral and social science research is an extremely contentious national issue. The purpose of this chapter is not to directly weigh in on this debate. Instead, it seeks to offer faculty and students (graduate and undergraduate) who wish to conduct oral history research some perspective on this very real problem. Several strategies will be suggested that may help in either eliminating IRB oversight altogether or at least creating a more acceptable middle ground.

TRYING TO REDEFINE RESEARCH

In recent years both the American Historical Association and the Oral History Association have sought to free up most oral history research from IRB oversight by lobbying the Office for Human Research Protections (OHRP), the federal agency that is charged with monitoring institutional compliance with the Common Rule. This agency, which is housed in the U.S. Department of Health and Human Services (HHS), regularly issues policy guidelines to clarify regulations. The policy guideline sought by the AHA and OHA was issued by OHRP in 2003. It categorically stated that oral history interviews did not contribute to "generalizable knowledge" as defined in the Common Rule. Since such contributions are what usually necessitate IRB review, oral history projects "... can be excluded from institutional review board (IRB) oversight because they do not involve research as defined by HHS regulations."[4] The proponents of this policy believed that it would allow IRBs to effectively distinguish between the methodology of oral history and other research approaches that should be regulated because they involve "a systematic investigation, including research development, testing and evaluation, designed to develop or contribute to generalizable knowledge."[5] The tipping point, of course, was getting IRBs to agree that researchers using oral history "do not reach generalizable principles of historical social development, nor do they seek underlying principles or laws of nature that have predictive value and can be applied to other circumstances for the purposes of controlling outcomes."[6]

It seemed patently obvious to the supporters of the OHRP policy statement that oral history interviews conducted by most qualitative researchers were readily distinguishable from such systematic investigation. The Oral History Association's definition of oral history makes this abundantly clear: "... a method of gathering and preserving historical information through recorded interviews with participants in past events and ways of life."[7] In other words, the end goal of an oral history interview is to capture a unique perspective or a specific past. Initially, spokespersons for the AHA and OHA voiced cautious optimism that IRBs would implement OHRP's policy statement. Unfortunately, only a handful of IRBs did so, and a national survey conducted in 2006 by the American Historical Association indicated that the statement had had little positive impact.[8] While IRBs were certainly aware of the OHRP policy statement, most appear to have either chosen to consider it as merely a recommendation or interpret the fine print in such a way as to support continued oversight of all oral history research.

THE IRB MIND-SET

One of the best ways to try to understand why the OHRP's policy statement on oral history has had so little impact and what can be done about it is to examine the IRB mind-set. To do this effectively, a bit of conjecture is required. Such conjecture is, of course, grounded on the presumption that IRBs are indeed risk-aversive and will always err on the side of some level of oversight rather than categorically declare that a certain type of research is exempt. Furthermore, a careful reading of the policy statement makes it readily apparent that OHRP never proposed a blanket exemption. This is apparent from the first word in the opening sentence: "Most oral history interviewing projects are not subject to...."[9] While this caveat is not only never clarified, it is reinforced in the concluding paragraph of the policy: "For these reasons, then, oral history interviewing, in general, does not meet the regulatory definition of research as articulated in 45 CFR part 46."[10] So even if the chair of an IRB wishes to faithfully implement this policy it would seem that he or she must still develop a procedure to determine what kinds of oral history are in the "most" or "in general" category and which are not.

Another important mind-set consideration is the often huge divide between the research training of IRB members and human research protection program administrators and that of the faculty and students in the social sciences and humanities. The "hard science" backgrounds of most IRB members is a given. To expect that even an IRB that is assigned oversight of research proposals only from the social sciences and humanities will be well informed about how and why oral history should be considered exempt is naïve. E. Taylor Atkins, a historian, and one of the leading advocates of working with and educating IRBs as opposed to confronting them, admitted his frustration after he attended a panel in 2006 on ethnographic research methods at the national PRIM&R Conference (Public Responsibility in Medicine and Research). He came away appalled by the "persistent ignorance" of IRB administrators and board members about the special needs of qualitative researchers such as oral historians.[11] To his credit, he still strongly encourages faculty members from the social sciences and humanities to volunteer to serve on IRBs and to embrace rather than resist the ethical training that all researchers must go through on their campuses.

In 2006 the influential American Association of University Professors (AAUP) issued a major report on Institutional Review Boards and academic freedom. One of the report's strongest recommendations was that qualitative research methods, including oral history, be given a blanket exemption from IRB review. The report was unequivocal on this issue, "that research on autonomous adults whose methodology consists entirely of collecting data by surveys, conducting interviews, or observing behavior in public places be exempt from the requirement of IRB—straightforwardly exempt, with no proviso, and no requirement of IRB approval of the exemption."[12] Unfortunately, even this unqualified recommendation from the nation's largest organization of college professors has fallen on deaf ears.

A letter in response to the AAUP's recommendation from the chair of the IRB at the University of California, Santa Cruz, is very instructive on the risk-related concerns that human subject research protection programs in general have when asked to designate qualitative research like oral history as nonreviewable. Bruce Bridgeman, a professor of psychology and psychobiology, believed that the AAUP's recommendation was based on "some misunderstanding of the challenges facing IRBs and universities in managing research."[13] As he saw it, a limited review of such research by an IRB chair was necessary "because the principal investigator has a vested interest in minimizing a project's apparent risk." Such risk comes from ". . . many proposals for surveys and interviews involving illegal activities, such as drug use. . . . ," and other studies involving "undocumented workers."[14] Though he recognized that some IRBs often place too many restrictions on "unproblematic" studies, he wrote, "In borderline cases, a review is necessary because of the vulnerability to lawsuits, no matter how frivolous. Defending any lawsuit is expensive and traumatic to the principle investigator. Approval by a recognized university entity transfers legal responsibility to the university."[15] Is this an overly alarmist position? Perhaps. Most IRBs are not so fearful of lawsuits, but they are by nature very cautious creatures.

THE BEST APPROACHES TO THE IRB

What is the best path to take either to eliminate all IRB oversight of oral history research or at least to reduce such review to a minimally intrusive level? Whether this is the first time such an attempt has been made or a repeat effort, the first step should be to provide the IRB with as much background and supporting information as you can possibly amass. The following checklist may be helpful in doing this:

1. Prepare a guide that thoroughly explains the methodology of oral history as a research tool.
2. Develop a bibliography of oral history sources, including examples of similar oral history research that has been published and/or is housed in libraries or archives.
3. Submit and explain how the *Evaluation Guidelines/Principles and Standards* of the Oral History Association guides your project.
4. Describe your own training and work in oral history.

5. If there is enough activity, have your department create a committee to review all proposed oral history research.
6. Present the IRB with examples of policies at other universities that either provide a blanket exemption for oral research or provide very nonobtrusive ways of clearing such research.

Fortunately, policies currently in place at three major universities are very instructive in the context of No. 6. At the University of Michigan, the Human Research Protection Program lists activities that do and do not constitute human subjects research under the Common Rule. Oral History appears on the activities list with a prominent "NO" beside the description of this activity. To qualify as not constituting human subject research, the oral history must consist of:

> interviews with sources (knowledgeable people) to supplement written documents and artifacts in attempting to preserve information about past events so long as: (i) they focus exclusively on past events; (ii) they are conducted to understand or explain a particular past or unique event in history; and (iii) the anonymity of the narrators is not preserved. Social Scientists other than historians may conduct research that meets these criteria and historians may conduct research that does not meet these criteria.[16]

Following the "NO" is the statement "(but exercise of professional ethics is expected)." There is no provision anywhere else in the University of Michigan Human Research Protection Program's operations manual that directs researchers using oral history even to notify an IRB if their project fits this definition. The only way that a researcher at the University of Michigan employing oral history comes in for any IRB consideration is if he or she receives funding from a federal agency that operates under the Common Rule or if the researcher initiates contact. In the former situation, the only requirement would be to complete the university's online research certification program. This course includes modules on human subject protection and research administration and reporting. The latter scenario apparently comes about when a researcher is unclear whether the proposed interviewees or the subject matter fit the definition for exclusion.[17] A project on the history of undocumented aliens in Ann Arbor, for example, most likely would be the kind of research that would prompt a researcher to contact the IRB for approval.

The Office of Research Support and Compliance at the University of Texas also has determined that oral history research should be excluded from review. The policy statement that OHRP issued in 2003 is cited as the basis for this exclusion. If the oral history research is "a method of gathering and preserving historical information through recorded interviews with participants about past events and ways of life..." then it is excluded from IRB review.[18] A list of the departments most likely to be affected by this exclusion of oral history research is also provided: American Studies, Anthropology, Geography, Government, History, Latin American Studies, Middle Eastern Studies, Music, and Theater/Dance. However, faculty and graduate students in these departments are still expected to fill out an application claiming this exemption and submit it to the appropriate IRB chair. Although in most cases that is as far as the review process goes, the chair does have the authority to determine that either the proposed interviewees or the subject matter does not fit under the oral history exclusion and that more direct IRB review is needed. This policy, in effect, directly implements the 2003 OHRP policy statement on oral history research. That is, to find out what constitutes "most" oral history research for exclusion purposes, you must provide a minimal level of scrutiny.

The third major university that construes oral history as nonreviewable research is Columbia. The statement that implements this policy offers the fullest and best articulation of why oral history research should be excluded from IRB review. While Columbia's statement, like that of the University of Texas, grounds its exemption on OHRP's policy statement, it also relies heavily on the work and reputation of the Oral History Research Office (OHRO). But the role of the OHRO in support of this policy is also a proactive one. All faculty and students at Columbia who wish to do oral history research are to first consult with either the OHRO or the IRB to determine if the proposed interview project is excluded from IRB oversight.[19] Columbia's IRB policy statement presumes that "oral history interviews, that only document specific historical events or the experiences of individuals or communities over different time periods would not constitute 'human subject research' as they would not support or lead to the development of a hypothesis in a manner that would have predictive value."[20] If the OHRO or the IRB, however, determines that the proposed oral history research does not fit the exclusionary policy statement, the IRB chair would then have to determine whether it posed less than minimum risk and thus could be treated as exempt research.[21]

To aid researchers planning to do oral history, Columbia's policy statement provides two hypothetical examples of projects together with thoughtful explanations of why one would be excluded and the other require IRB review. The first example presents a graduate student who is writing a dissertation on the long-term social impact of the Vietnam War on American culture. Part of the research will involve life histories of veterans to document the broader meaning of the war in their lives. The resulting interviews will be donated to the Veterans History Project at the Library of Congress. A separate "Rationale" follows the example, explaining that the project does not require IRB approval because "...the information collected from the interviews is not a systematic investigation (it is not intended to address a hypothesis)."[22]

A second example, also dealing with the Vietnam War, presents a faculty member who is doing a long-term study of Post Traumatic Stress Disorder (PTSD) in veterans. The researcher plans to work with an existing PTSD support group to secure interviews with some of the members. One stated goal of the research is to develop assessments of what type of exposure to war is most likely to produce PTSD. One of the conditions required by the support group is that all participants will remain anonymous. The separate "Rationale" following this example explains that this project does require IRB approval because ". . . the information collected from the interviewees will be designed to contribute to generalizable knowledge."[23] The fact that the veterans are to remain anonymous was not a factor in the determination that this is IRB-reviewable research.

Conclusion

A 2007 article in the *New York Times* painted a bleak picture of the extent to which qualitative research done by faculty and students from the social sciences and humanities is forced to undergo time-consuming and needless oversight by IRBs. In the article, Bernard A. Schwetz, the director of the Office for Human Research Protection (OHRP), admitted that clearer guidelines from his office might help IRBs to be less intrusive. In the same breath, however, he still contended that human subjects must always be protected from any dangers associated with non-medical research: "I think it's naïve to say there isn't any risk."[24]

It is likewise naïve to assume that researchers on university and college campuses across the nation who wish to employ oral history will be freed from IRB oversight any time soon. But education and negotiation are the methods most likely to secure the least invasive IRB oversight. It also helps to remember that most IRB determinations are not readily reviewable. There is no formal appeals process on most campuses.[25] So unless you are willing to enter into a protracted confrontation, which might even involve filing a complaint with the Office for Human Research Protection (OHRP), your best bet is to educate and negotiate. While the complete exclusion policies at Columbia and Michigan are still the exceptions rather than the rule, they would certainly be the best models to try to emulate. Failing that, plan B would be to bring the University of Texas model to your campus.

| 9 |

Is There a Duty to Report a Crime?

It happens so rarely that even in-depth oral history workshops and graduate oral history courses never broach the subject. This rarity occurs when an interviewee either admits to an interviewer that he or she committed a crime or names someone else as the perpetrator. If the interviewee is elderly, the admission or revelation is most likely so far in the past that it no longer matters except to the narrator. But what if the interviewee is not an octogenarian but a much younger individual and the crime that he or she is relating is neither distant nor dated? Does an oral history interviewer have any legal duty to report what he or she was told and recorded? If there is no legal duty is there an ethical one?

One could construct any number of hypothetical examples of this sort of stunning revelation but a handful of oral historians have readily admitted on H-NET/OHA, the oral history listserv, to being privy to such admissions and/or accusations. The crimes that they mention included fraudulent land use claims, war crimes, and election fraud. One oral historian during a public presentation even claimed that one of his interviewee's had confessed to a murder.[1]

The suggestions from other oral historians on the listserv as to how to handle such revelations focused primarily on remedial steps such as: whether to immediately turn off the tape recorder, to warn the interviewee that such an admission was ill-advised, or to urge him or her to delete that information from the interview. While all of these responses were well intended, they did not address the fundamental issue here: is an interviewer who learns of the commission of a crime under any legal duty to report this information to the proper authorities?

In other words, once you know, what if anything should you or must you do? This is a mixed question of law and ethics.

Societal versus Legal Expectations

Despite Americans' reputation for helping each other, both collectively and individually, the American legal system traditionally has not imposed liability, either civil or criminal, on individuals for their failure to render aid, promptly report, or actually rescue someone in distress.[2] In fact, greater liability often occurs when a Good Samaritan is somehow negligent in his or her rescue effort. In recent decades, however, the legal responsibilities placed on individuals who are at the scene of a crime or accident have been noticeably increasing. For example, a substantial number of states have passed legislation requiring citizens to report or render assistance to victims of accidents and serious crimes. Although there are significant variations from state to state, Texas, for example, recently criminalized the failure of any citizen who witnesses the commission of a serious crime to immediately report it to the police unless he or she would place themselves in danger of serious bodily harm by doing so or it was reasonable to assume someone else had made the required report.[3] These types of laws obviously apply only to eyewitnesses but are worth noting because they put into perspective the legal duty that can emerge when a person receives after the fact information about the commission of a felony. This offense, which is called misprision of felony, is the one that oral historians need to be aware of whenever an interviewee admits to a past crime or accuses another of committing such an offense.

Federal Misprision of Felony

The origins of this crime go back to medieval England but misprision of felony was included in the first federal criminal code in 1790, and today individuals are still being charged and convicted of this offense: "Whoever, having knowledge of the actual commission of a felony cognizable by a court of the United States, conceals and does not as soon as possible make known the same to some judge or other person in civil or military authority under the United States, shall be fined under this title or imprisoned not more than three years or both."[4]

Like all criminal offenses, key elements must be proven beyond a reasonable doubt before a conviction can be secured. For federal misprision of felony these elements are:

1. the commission and completion of a felony;
2. the defendant's knowledge of that fact;
3. failure of the defendant to notify the proper authority;
4. some affirmative step by the defendant to conceal the felony.[5]

The key elements for the purposes of this discussion are Nos. 2, 3, and 4. Both case law and respected authorities are in agreement that there must first be actual knowledge that a crime was committed, No. 2. Something more than rumor or innuendo is required. Failure to provide the proper authorities with the information, No. 3, must always be accompanied by some form of concealment, No. 4. In other words, a person who learns about a crime but merely keeps the information to himself or herself—this is not enough. He or she must also make untruthful statements, hide evidence, or actively shield the perpetrator to satisfy No. 4. A 2008 case, *In re Calonge,* effectively illustrates this affirmative requirement. Gloria Calonge, the defendant, drafted and mailed a letter to the U.S. Citizenship and Immigration Service to cover up a fraudulent certificate of employment that had been previously submitted. Because she knew that the employment certificate was a fraud, writing a letter in her capacity as an attorney constituted the type of concealment that is needed to satisfy element No. 4.[6]

STATE MISPRISION OF FELONY

Today, the vast majority of states do not have a misprision of felony offense in their criminal codes. For a variety of reasons, this offense was either never recognized or it has been amended so as to apply only to persons who are eyewitnesses to the commission of a violent felony.[7] A closer look at several states that do recognize the offense is instructive. South Carolina is one of the states in which failure to disclose knowledge of crimes to authorities is still prosecuted. In 1980 an eyewitness to a murder and robbery in Charleston was convicted of this offense after he lied to the police both about whether he had been at the scene where the crime occurred and whether he observed anything. Independent witnesses had identified him and placed him in a position to observe the crime prior to his denials to the police. He was convicted of misprision of felony.[8]

Although the fact pattern of this case has no connection to the work that oral historians do, it and similar prosecutions apparently prompted a member of the South Carolina House of Representatives a decade later to request an opinion from the attorney general on the reporting obligations of researchers who were conducting a study entitled "Substance Abuse in South Carolina Black Communities." He raised two questions: "Can a researcher be compelled to testify regarding alleged violations of criminal law which the researcher acquires while accumulating data? Is a researcher obligated to come forward and report criminal activity, the knowledge of which the researcher acquires while accumulating data?"[9] Although the first question is certainly important to oral historians, the second question is the crucial one for this discussion. The attorney general's opinion addressed it as a mixed question of law and morality. He noted that "each individual must be guided by his own conscience; nevertheless, anyone who acts affirmatively to conceal a criminal undertaking could be committing the crime of misprision of felony."[10] But after reviewing the elements of misprision of felony in South Carolina in relation to the projected role of the researchers, the opinion concluded, "Thus, it appears that the mere failure of a researcher to come forward, without some affirmative act to conceal, would not be misprision of felony.[11]

Ohio and South Dakota are two other states that recognize the offense, but unlike South Carolina they have directly incorporated it into their statutes. Both these statutes are written broadly enough to raise the possibility that an oral historian who learns of a past crime could be prosecuted for failing to come forward. The South Dakota statute provides: "Any person who, having knowledge which is not privileged, of the commission of a felony, conceals the same, or does not immediately disclose such felony with the name of the perpetrator thereof, and all facts in relation thereto, to proper authorities, shall be guilty of misprision of felony."[12] The statute does not, however, require anyone to report the commission of a misdemeanor, which is a less serious crime than a felony and generally results in a fine and/or less than one year of imprisonment.

The Ohio statute simply states that "no person, knowing that a felony has been or is being committed, shall knowingly fail to report such information to law enforcement authorities."[13] As one learned commentator noted, "Ohio's statute is unambiguous in making criminal an omission to report a felony."[14] This statute, however, does not apply to privileged communications with attorneys, doctors, licensed psychologists, drug counselors, and confidential clergy-parishioner counseling. There are no published cases indicating that either of these two state statutes has ever been used to prosecute a researcher or anyone else who received information about a past felony and simply failed to report it.

CONFESSION VERSUS ACCUSATION

Before turning to the ethical side of this issue, another factor needs to be addressed, namely, whether an interviewee personally admits committing a past criminal offense or simply accuses another of doing so. The language of the federal misprision of felony statute clearly specifies that there must be "actual knowledge" of the commission of a felony. The personal admission of an interviewee would seemingly satisfy this requirement. An accusation, however, would be far weaker if the narrator did not actually witness the crime and thus did not have "actual knowledge" but only learned about it from someone else (in which case it would be hearsay).

LEGAL DUTY?

Legally there is only the remotest possibility that a researcher, who learned of a previously committed crime and did not come forward, would be charged with misprision of a felony. If the information was about a federal crime, case law clearly demonstrates that whoever received such information would not be chargeable unless he or she took some affirmative action to prevent disclosure. The mere act of receiving such information during the course of one's research would not suffice. Oral historians in Ohio and South Dakota who learn of a past criminal act are in a somewhat more ambiguous situation because of the very expansive wording of the misprision of felony statutes in these states. But even this observation must be hedged by other considerations. Whether the offense can still be prosecuted is one important factor. All federal and state criminal offenses are subject to statute of limitations. These are the time periods during which a criminal offense must be prosecuted. If these time limits are not met, the alleged perpetrator of a crime cannot be prosecuted. In Wisconsin, for example, criminal offenses like robbery and burglary must be prosecuted within six years from the date upon which the crime was committed. For homicides, however, there is no statute of limitations.[15] Another consideration is whether the crime in question was a felony or misdemeanor. The latter type of offense is a lesser crime like criminal damage to property or resisting arrest. Because such offenses are not felonies, they are not the type of reportable crimes that are envisioned by either the federal or misprision of felony statutes in Ohio and South Dakota.

PROFESSIONAL ETHICS?

The discussion thus far has focused solely on whether there is a legal duty to report a crime. It is also important to consider this question from the vantage point of both professional and personal ethics. The *Principles and Standards* of the Oral History Association does not directly address this issue beyond urging oral historians "to maintain the highest professional standards in the conduct of their work."[16] The *Principles and Standards* does, however, recommend that "the standards of the various disciplines to which they are affiliated" be followed.[17] While this statement may be seen as ducking the issue, it does recognize that the vast majority of oral historians are simply users of the methodology. The American Historical Association, American Sociological Association, American Anthropological Association, and American Folklore Society all have statements of ethical conduct in research that can be found on their Web sites. While none of these professional standards address the duty to report a crime question directly, the American Sociological Association (ASA) indirectly considers it within the context of confidentiality. The section on Maintaining Confidentiality provides, "Confidential information provided by research participants, students, employees, clients, or others is treated as such by sociologists even if there is no legal protection or privilege to do so."[18] The section on Limits of Confidentiality instructs sociologists to ". . . inform themselves fully about laws and rules which may limit or alter guarantees of confidentiality."[19] Subsection (b) goes on to warn sociologists that "unanticipated circumstances whether they become aware of information that is clearly health or life threatening. . . . may force them to balance any guarantees of confidentiality with other principles in the Code of Ethics and applicable laws."[20] While 11.02 (b) clearly focuses on very contemporaneous threats or crimes, Subsection (a) seems to alert sociologists to the need to be informed about state and federal laws that may require them to report information regarding a past crime.

Obviously, pledges of confidentiality in general certainly encourage research subjects to be more inclined to "tell all." Thus the ASA *Code of Ethics* seeks to put sociologists on notice that if they get into this type of situation, they should educate themselves regarding state and federal laws that might at some point impose on them a legal duty to breach a pledge of confidentiality.

Personal Ethics?

As Valerie Yow, a strong advocate for professional ethics in oral history research aptly notes, "Ethical issues, however, are even more difficult to solve than legal issues."[21] This would certainly be the case if one is faced with the decision about whether to report a past crime. Even if there is no clear-cut legal duty to report a past crime, as the U.S. Supreme Court notes, "Gross indifference to the duty to report known criminal behavior remains a badge of irresponsible citizenship."[22] So if an oral historian believes that he or she is morally bound to share with local authorities either the confession of an interviewee or his or her criminal accusation against someone else, this would be a matter of personal ethics. If one's moral compass leads to a decision to bring such information to the attention of the authorities, it would still be advisable to first try and corroborate the interviewee's confession or accusation before passing it on. Such corroboration is even more important if the interviewee has accused someone else of committing a crime. Unless the criminal act was one that was never discovered, a check of local newspaper files should be made to determine whether the reputed crime did indeed happen and along the lines that the interviewee claimed. Finally, before going to the police, it is advisable to ascertain that the alleged crime is indeed a felony and that prosecution of the perpetrator is not barred by a statute of limitations.

Conclusion

| | |

Anticipation and prevention are the two major watchwords of this book. Such emphasis on preventative law reflects a rapidly growing trend in all walks of life. A seemingly endless number of seminars and publications, for example, are available to help executives and human resource directors avoid legally unsound practices and policies. Prevention is even becoming more prevalent in general public education efforts. The Washington State Bar Association's Council on Public Legal Education, for example, maintains a Web site appropriately entitled *lawforWA.org*. Visitors to this Web site who click on the "Prevent and Solve Legal Problems" link are immediately informed that they "... will find resources for preventing common legal problems and for solving them if they exist." This is no empty promise. Thirty-four legal subtopics from administrative law to youth are available and each one provides a wealth of helpful resources to avoid legal problems.

Oral historians, of course, should always be active supporters of preventative law. Stated in more colloquial terms, an ounce of prevention is better than a pound of cure. And indeed it is if the cure involves paying legal fees, court costs, monetary damages, and even harming the reputation of the program. Even a successful defense against a lawsuit can be expensive, time-consuming, and have unpleasant public relations consequences. The overriding message of this book is that preventative law is the best legal protection that an individual or program can invest in.

Whenever I conduct workshops on legal issues involving oral history, I always present several hypothetical scenarios and then ask the attendees to think about how they might respond if it was their program or research that was in the crosshairs. My purpose in doing this is not only to come up with a sound legal strategy for each scenario but also to bring up a more fundamental issue, namely, whether there is a general plan in place to both prevent troublesome legal problems from arising and how to address them if they do. Such a contingency plan should not only include knowing whom to turn to for legal assistance but also involve a continuing legal assessment of both existing procedures and new initiatives.

Oral historians are fortunate that so few legal challenges have arisen to date. Such good fortune, however, must not foster a false sense of security or complacency. The mind boggling expansion in the use of oral history and the increasing emphasis on more contemporary and controversial subjects will inevitably bring more legal challenges and lawsuits in their wake. The potential legal pitfalls outlined in this book are very real. Oral historians should in most instances, however, be able to continue to stay out of court by observing a few simple rules:

1. Develop and maintain the strongest possible professional ethics based on the *Evaluation Guidelines/Principles and Standards* of the Oral History Association.
2. Anticipate potential legal problems and implement appropriate preventative measures.
3. Alert your staff to all potential areas of liability. If you work alone, then educate yourself.
4. Keep up-to-date on new legal developments just like you do with new equipment and scholarship.
5. Do not let financial considerations deter you from consulting a lawyer. Remember, preventative law is always far less expensive, nerve-wracking, and time-consuming than litigation.

| APPENDIX 1 |

Sample Legal Release Forms

These forms are presented for informational purposes only. Some of the forms contain the names of fictitious Wisconsin entities for the sole purpose of illustration. In drafting these forms, no attempt was made to try and incorporate additional legal requirements that individual states may have for either deeds of gift or contracts. Anyone wishing to utilize any of these sample agreements should first consult with a knowledgeable attorney.

1. Deed of Gift
2. Deed of Gift with Restrictions
3. Contractual Agreement
4. Contractual Agreement with Restrictions
5. Deed of Gift: Volunteer Interviewer
6. Deed of Gift: Independent Researcher
7. Deed of Gift: Interviewer as Joint Author
8. Deed of Gift: Next of Kin
9. IRB Consent Form
10. IRB Consent Form & Deed of Gift
11. Permission to Use: Middle & High School
12. Work-Made-for-Hire Agreement
13. Assignment of Copyright in a Work Intended as a Work-Made-for-Hire

No. 1
Deed of Gift

The mission of the Longview Historical Center is to document the history of Northern Wisconsin. An important part of this effort is the collection of oral history interviews with knowledgeable individuals from all walks of life. In order for your interview/s to be placed in the Center's archive for future historical use, it will be necessary for you to sign this gift agreement. Before doing so, you should read it carefully and ask any questions you may have regarding its terms and conditions.

I,_____ [interviewee], of_____[address, city, state, zip code], herein permanently donate and convey my oral history interview/s to the Longview Historical Center. In making this gift, I understand that I am conveying all right, title, and interest in copyright to the Center. In return, the Center grants me a nonexclusive license to utilize my interview/s during my lifetime. I also grant to the Center the right to use my name and likeness in any promotional materials for publications or projects.

I further understand that I will have the opportunity to review and edit my interview/s before it is/they are made available for historical research whether in audio/video and/or transcript form. The Center will then make my interview/s available for research without restriction. Future uses may include quotation and publication or broadcast in any media, including the Internet.

_____   _____
Interviewee   Interviewer or Agent

_____   _____
Date   Date

No. 2
DEED OF GIFT WITH RESTRICTIONS

The mission of the Longview Historical Center is to document the history of Northern Wisconsin. An important part of this effort is the collection of oral history interviews with knowledgeable individuals from all walks of life. In order for your interview/s to be placed in the Center's archive for future historical use, it will be necessary for you to sign this gift agreement. Before doing so, you should read it carefully and ask any questions you may have regarding its terms and conditions.

I,_____[interviewee], of_____ [address, city, state, zip code] herein permanently donate and convey to the Longview Historical Center my oral history interview/s. In making this gift, I understand that I am conveying all right, title, and interest in copyright to the Longview Historical Center. In return, the Center grants to me a nonexclusive license to utilize my interview/s during my lifetime. I also grant to the Center the right to use my name and likeness in any promotional materials for publications or projects.

I further understand that I will have an opportunity to review and edit my interview/s before it is/they are made available for historical research whether in audio/video and/or transcript form. The Center will then make my interview/s available to researchers subject to the following restriction/s. Future uses may include quotation and publication or broadcast in any media, including the Internet.

Restrictions

_____I wish to close my interviews until_____

_____I wish to close specific portions of my interview/s until_____

_____I wish to restrict access to on-site users until_____

_____No researcher may quote from my interview/s without my permission until _____

_____I wish to be identified by a pseudonym and have all references from which my iden-
      tity could be known redacted until_____

The Center agrees to take all reasonable steps to honor my restrictions. I understand, however, that the Center may not be able to uphold my restriction/s against either a freedom of information request or a subpoena.

_____   _____
Interviewee   Interviewer or Agent

_____   _____
Date   Date

No. 3
Contractual Agreement

The mission of the U.S. Army History Center is to document and preserve the individual histories of U.S. Army personnel in recent wars and conflicts. The goal of the Desert Storm Oral History Project is to record the experiences of participants in this war. To deposit your interview/s with the Center, it will be necessary for you to sign this agreement. Before doing so, you should carefully read it and ask any questions you may have regarding its terms and conditions.

In consideration for the audio and/or video recording, editing, processing and archiving of my interview/s by the Desert Storm Oral History Project,

I_____[interviewee], of_____ [address, city, state, zip code] herein permanently transfer to the U.S. Army History Center my interview/s. In doing so I understand that I am conveying all right, title, and interest in copyright to the Center. In return, the Center grants to me a nonexclusive license to utilize my interview/s during my lifetime. I also grant the Center the right to use my name and likeness in any promotional materials for publications or projects.

I understand that I will have the opportunity to review and edit my interview/s before it is/they are made available for historical research whether in audio/video and/or transcript form. The Center will then make my interview/s available for research without restriction. Future uses may include quotation and publication or broadcast in any media, including the Internet.

_____   _____
Interviewee   Interviewer or Agent

_____   _____
Date   Date

No. 4
CONTRACTUAL AGREEMENT WITH RESTRICTIONS

The mission of the U.S. Army History Center is to document and preserve the individual histories of U.S. Army personnel in recent wars and conflicts. The goal of the Desert Storm Oral History Project is to record the experiences of participants in this war. To deposit your interview/s with the Center, it will be necessary for you to sign this agreement. Before doing so, you should carefully read it and ask any questions you may have regarding its terms and conditions.

In consideration for the audio and/or video recording, editing, processing and archiving of my interview/s by the Desert Storm Oral History Project, I_____ [name] of_____ [address, city, state, zip code] herein permanently transfer to the U.S. Army History Center my interview/s. In doing so I understand that I am conveying all right, title, and interest in copyright to the Center. In return the Center grants to me a nonexclusive license to utilize my interview/s during my lifetime. I also grant the Center the right to use my name and likeness in any promotional materials for publications or projects.

I further understand that I will have the opportunity to review and edit my interview/s before it is/they are made available for historical research whether in audio/video and/or transcript from. The Center will then make my interview/s available for research subject to the following restriction/s. Future uses may include quotation and publication or broadcast in any media, including the Internet.

Restrictions

_____I wish to close my interviews until_____

_____I wish to close specific portions of my interviews until_____

_____I wish to restrict access to on-site users until_____

_____No researcher may quote from my interview/s without my permission until_____

_____I wish to be identified by a pseudonym and have all references from which my identity could be known redacted until_____

The Center agrees to take all reasonable steps to honor my restrictions. I understand, however, that the Center may not be able to uphold my restriction/s against either a freedom of information request or a subpoena.

_____   _____
Interviewee   Interviewer or Agent

_____   _____
Date   Date

No. 5
DEED OF GIFT: VOLUNTEER INTERVIEWER

The Milwaukee Neighborhoods Project is dedicated to the preservation of historic neigh-borhoods. To this end, oral history interviews are being conducted with elderly Milwau-keeans throughout the City. This project is partially funded by a grant from the Wisconsin Humanities Council and sustained for the most part by the work of volunteers. To ensure that the interview/s that you conduct as a volunteer interviewer can be archived and used for research, you are asked to sign the following agreement. Before doing so, you should carefully read it and ask any questions regarding its terms and conditions.

I_____[interviewer] do herein permanently donate and convey all interviews that I conduct for the Milwaukee Neighborhoods Project to the Milwaukee Historical Society. In making this gift, I understand that I am conveying all right, title, and interest in copyright that I might hold as a joint author to the Society.

I understand that I will have the opportunity to review the interview/s before it is/they are made available for historical research whether in audio/video and/or transcript from. The Society will then make the interview/s available to researchers without restrictions. Future uses may include quotation and publication or broadcast in any media, including the Internet.

_____   _____
Project Director   Interviewer

_____   _____
Date   Date

No. 6
DEED OF GIFT: INDEPENDENT RESEARCHER

The Biography of Randall Towns Project
Ruth Allen Bates, Ph.D.

I am currently doing research for a biography on Randall Towns.

An important part of my research is the oral history interviews I am conducting with individuals who had significant contact with Mr. Towns during the course of his life. The purpose of the following agreement is to allow me to utilize your interview in my book and subsequently to donate it to a library or archive so that other researchers may be able to benefit from your historical recollections. Please read the agreement carefully before you sign it and feel free to ask any questions you may have regarding its terms and conditions.

I_____[interviewee]   of_____
[address, city, state, zip code] do herein permanently donate and convey my oral history interview and other written material as noted, _____ to Ruth Allen Bates. In making this gift, I understand that I am assigning all right, title, and interest in copyright to Dr. Bates. By virtue of this assignment, Dr. Bates will have the right to freely use my interview/s and any other written materials specified above in her biography.

I further understand that once this study is completed, she will donate my interview and any written materials to an appropriate archive or library so that other researchers may be able to utilize them. This donation will include the transfer of all interest in copyright that I herein assigned. Dr. Bates agrees in turn to inform me of the library or archive that will ultimately be the repository of my interview/s and materials.

_____   _____
Interviewee   Dr. Ruth Allen Bates

_____   _____
Date   Date

No. 7

DEED OF GIFT: INTERVIEWER AS JOINT AUTHOR

I_____,[interviewer] who conducted interviews for the _____ [program/project] with_____ [interviewee] on or about_____[date], for which no legal releases were executed, do herein permanently donate and convey said interview/s to the_____[archive/library]. In doing so, I understand that the interview/s I conducted with _____ [interviewee] will be made available to researchers and may be quoted, published, or broadcast in any media, including the Internet that the_____ [archive/library] shall deem appropriate.

In making this gift, I fully understand that I am conveying all right, title, and interest in copyright which I have or may be deemed to have in the interview/s as a joint author. I further recognize the joint authorship in copyright that_____ [interviewee or his/her next of kin] holds in the interview/s. In consideration for my assignment of copyright, the _____[archive/library] agrees to release me from any claim that might arise from profits that are derived from the commercial use of the interview/s with_____ [interviewee].

_____   _____
Interviewer   Agent

_____   _____
Date   Date

No. 8
DEED OF GIFT: NEXT OF KIN

In accordance with the willing participation of_____ [name of interviewee], in the _____[name of oral history project or program] on_____[date], at which time he/she provided interview/s to _____[name of receiving group or individual] for which no legal release was executed. As next of kin, I_____,[name & relationship] herein do permanently donate and convey to the _____ [name of archive/library] the interview/s with _____ [name of interviewee]. In doing so I understand that_____ interview/s will be made available to researchers and may be quoted, published, and broadcast in any media including the Internet.

I further acknowledge in making this gift that I am conveying all right, title, and interest in copyright to _____ interview/s [name of interviewee] to _____[archive or library].

_____

Next of Kin

_____

Date

_____

Authorized Agent

_____

Date

No. 9
IRB Consent Form
Lake Michigan University
Laurie Bonner, History

"The Championship Years: Women's Basketball, 1992–2000"
I agree to be interviewed by Laurie Bonner for her dissertation. I understand that she is interviewing key players, coaches, and support personnel. I further understand that this consent form is intended to fully inform me of what I am being asked to do and my rights as a human subject.

Research Procedure
The interview will be recorded. It will last somewhere between 1 and 2 hours. If the researcher finds that more interview time is needed, she will work out a suitable time and date for this. Once my interview is completed, it will be edited and transcribed. I will be given an opportunity to make changes to my interview before a final transcript is completed. No one except Laurie Bonner will be able to access my interview until the final transcript is finished. After I have given my approval to the final transcript, I will then be asked to sign a deed of gift conveying my interview to the Lake Michigan University Sports History Archive.

Confidentiality
Because the purpose of the interview is to secure specific factual information and insights about the greatest era in women's basketball at Lake Michigan University, allowing interviewees to remain anonymous is not an intended feature of this study. I do, however, have the right not to answer any questions that I consider uncomfortable or inappropriate. If the prospect of being personally identified in Ms. Bonner's dissertation, future publications, or in the interview is a concern at any time, I can either withdraw entirely from this study without any penalty or ask to be assigned a pseudonym, in which case all identifying information from my interview will be redacted.

Withdrawal without Prejudice
Participation in this study is strictly voluntary. Each interviewee is free to withdraw consent and cease all participation in this study at any time without any penalty whatsoever.

Risks and Benefits
There are no known risks or discomforts associated with your participation in this study. Although you may not receive any direct benefit from your participation, others may benefit from the knowledge that you provide to this study.

Costs and Payments
There is no cost to participate in this study nor will you be paid for your time. You will, however, receive a recording and transcript of your interview.

Questions and Concerns
If you have any questions or concerns about this study and the oral history interview process, you can call or e-mail Dr. John Ambrose, faculty advisor at (444) 765–4321 or jambrose@histLMU.edu. You may also contact the Human Subjects Research Office, at (444) 765–1234 or HSRO@LMU.edu.

Agreement

I have read the information contained in this consent form, and Laurie Bonner has offered to answer any questions I may have concerning the study. I hereby consent to participate in this study.

_____
Interviewee

_____
Date

_____
Researcher

_____
Date

No. 10
IRB Consent Form & Deed of Gift
Lake Michigan University
Zach Thomas, Sociology
"Lake Michigan Dock Workers: 1970–2000"

I have been invited to provide an oral history interview for this dissertation research. I understand that Zach Thomas is interviewing dock workers like me about their work experiences and association with the United Dock Workers Union. I also understand that he may use material from my interview in his dissertation and possibly in subsequent publications. I further understand that he wishes to donate my interview to the Lake Michigan University Labor Archive to assist future researchers. Unless I indicated otherwise, there will be no restrictions on the use of my interview by either Zach Thomas or the Labor Archive.

Research Methodology and Interviewee Rights

This recorded interview will be conducted in the form of a guided conversation and will last 1–2 hours. I understand that I will be free to decline to answer any question that I consider to be uncomfortable or inappropriate. Moreover, I will have the right to stop my interview at any time without any negative consequences. There are no foreseeable risks to my participation and the benefit is the increased knowledge about maritime workers and unions. There is no cost to my participation in this study, and I will not receive any compensation except for a recording of my interview. I further recognize that since my interview will be donated to the Labor Archive, there is no assumption of confidentiality unless I specifically request it.

Deed of Gift

I _____ do herein permanently donate and convey to the Lake Michigan University Labor Archive, my interview conducted on _____.
In making this gift, I understand that I am conveying all right, title, and interest in copyright to the Labor Archive. In return, the Archive grants me a nonexclusive license to utilize this interview during my lifetime.
I further understand that I will have the opportunity to review and edit my interview before it is made available for historical research whether in audio or transcript form. The Labor Archive will then make this interview available for research without restriction. Future uses may include quotation and publication or broadcast in any media, including the Internet.

Questions & Concerns

If you have any questions or concerns about this study or the oral history process, you can contact Dr. Blanche Rickey, faculty advisor at (777) 765-4321 or brickey@socLMU.edu. You may also contact the Human Subject Research Office at (777) 765-1234 or HSRO@ LMU.edu.

Consent Confirmation

I have read this agreement and Zach Thomas offered to answer any questions I may have concerning this study. He also informed me that I could request to remain anonymous if I chose to do so. I hereby consent to participate in this study.

_____   _____
Interviewee   Researcher

_____   _____
Date   Date

No. 11

PERMISSION TO USE: MIDDLE & HIGH SCHOOL

Students in my 11th Grade Social Studies class at Rib Mountain High School are conducting oral history interviews (audio or video taped) with community residents who experienced World War II either through military service or on the home front. Since you have agreed to be interviewed, it is important that you carefully read this agreement which explains how your interview will be used in this class project. If you have any questions regarding the terms and conditions of use, please ask your student interviewer or call me, Mr. Barry Bonduel at 555-5555.

I _____ [name of interviewee] of _____ [address]_____[city] _____[state & zip code] herein give my permission to_____[name of interviewer] to fully utilize my interview, including my name and likeness, in this class project. Once this project is completed, however, the audio or video recording of my interview as well as any transcript that was made shall be returned to me. No copies of my interview shall be retained by the interviewer, teacher, or school without my express permission.

_____   _____
Interviewee   Student Interviewer

_____   _____
Date   Date

No. 12

WORK-MADE-FOR-HIRE AGREEMENT

The Door County Historical Society is sponsoring a special project on historic resorts. In addition to collecting written sources, the Society wishes to conduct interviews with key individuals associated with the founding and/or management of these resorts. To that end, the Society wishes to hire _____, as an independent contractor to conduct interviews with the twelve (12) individuals whose names appear on the attached list. The purpose of this agreement is to outline the terms and conditions of your work including compensation and expenses.

Independent Contractor Status

For purposes of this agreement, you are an independent contractor and not an employee of the Society. In this capacity you agree to the following terms and rights consistent with your independent contractor status:

1. You have the right to perform services for others during the tenure of this agreement.
2. You have the sole right to control and direct the manner in which the interviews are conducted.
3. The Society will not withhold FICA from your compensation or make FICA payments on your behalf.
4. You are not eligible for employee benefits of any kind from the Society.

Copyright Ownership

The Door County Historical Society had conceived of any original work of authorship relating to the creation of oral histories with key individuals associated with historic resorts in Door County. Per this agreement, _____ is specially order and commissioned by the Society to conduct the interviews which are to be a part of the Society's archive as a collection, supplemental, or other category of work that is eligible to be treated as a Work-Made-for-Hire pursuant to 17 U.S.C. Sec. 101.
The Society and _____ intend that the copyrights in the interviews he/she conducts are to be owned by the Society who is to be considered the author of such interview/s as defined in 17 U.S.C. Sec. 201. _____ further agrees to present, explain, and secure signed deeds of gift for all of the interviews conducted pursuant to this agreement. The Society will supply the agreements for this purpose.

Compensation & Expenses

In consideration for the specially ordered and commissioned services addressed in this agreement, the Door County Historical Society agrees to pay _____, a flat fee of $250.00 for each recorded interview plus reasonable expenses for research, travel, and equipment. Payment will be made in two installments, with the first occurring upon receipt by the Society of the recordings and signed releases for six (6) of the interviewees and the remainder upon the completion and receipt of all interviews.

_____   _____
Independent Contractor   Agent Representative

_____   _____
Date   Date

No. 13

Assignment of Copyright in a Work Intended as a Work-Made-for-Hire

The Green County Historical Society is sponsoring a special project on historic Green Lake resorts. In addition to collecting written sources, the Society wishes to conduct interviews with key individuals associated with the founding and/or management of these resorts. To that end, the Society wishes to hire _____, as an independent contractor to conduct interviews with twelve (12) individuals whose names appear on the attached list. The purpose of this agreement is to outline the terms and conditions for your work, including compensation and expenses.

Independent Contractor Status

For purposes of this agreement you are considered to be an independent contractor and not an employee of the Society. In this capacity you agree to the following terms and rights consistent with your independent contractor status:

1. You have the right to perform services for others during the tenure of this agreement.
2. You have the sole right to control and direct the manner in which the interviews are conducted.
3. The Society will not withhold FICA from your compensation or make FICA payments on your behalf.
4. You are not eligible for employee benefits of any kind from the Society.

Copyright Ownership

The parties further agree that this specially commissioned or ordered work is a Work-Made-for-Hire, and that the Green County Historical Society for whom this work is prepared, shall own all right, title, and interest including copyright in said work.

The interviewer further agrees that in the event that the interviews he/she conducts are legally deemed not to be a Work-Made-for-Hire pursuant to 17 U.S.C. Sec (101), by virtue of this agreement he/she assigns to the Green County Historical Society all right, title, and interest including copyright that he may be entitled to claim as a joint author in these interviews. He/she further agrees to present, explain, and secure signed deeds of gift for the Society from each interview conducted pursuant to this agreement. The Society will provide the agreements for this purpose.

Compensation & Expenses

In consideration for the specially ordered and commissioned services addressed in this agreement, the Green County Historical Society agrees to pay _____, a flat fee of $250.00 for each recorded interview plus reasonable expenses for research, travel, and equipment. Payment will be made in two installments with the first coming upon receipt of the first six (6) interviews with signed releases and the remainder being paid upon the completion and receipt of the all interviews.

_____	_____
Independent Contractor	Agent/Representative
_____	_____
Date	Date

| APPENDIX 2 |

Oral History Evaluation Guidelines of the Oral History Association

Adopted 1989, Revised Sept. 2000

Foreword

Since its founding in 1967 the Oral History Association (OHA) has grappled constantly with developing and promoting professional standards for oral historians. This has been no easy task, given the creative, dynamic, and multidisciplinary nature of the field.

The OHA has sought to encourage the creation of recorded interviews that are as complete, verifiable, and usable as possible, and to discourage both inadequate interviewing and the misuse of history. Yet it recognizes that oral historians cannot afford to suppress ingenuity and inspiration nor to ignore new developments in scholarship and technology.

The OHA issued its first "goals and guidelines" in 1968, broadly stating the principles, rights, and obligations that all interviewees, interviewers, and sponsoring institutions needed to take into consideration. Then in 1979, at the prompting of various granting agencies, leaders of the OHA met at the Wingspread Conference Center in Racine, Wisconsin, to produce a set of "evaluation guidelines." These guidelines have since provided invaluable assistance to oral history projects of all sizes and purposes. Organized in checklist form, they offered reminders of the myriad of issues involved in conducting, processing, and preserving oral history interviews. Not every guideline applied to every project, but taken together they provided a common ground for dialogue among oral historians.

Over the next decade, new issues arose. When the need for revision of the earlier guidelines became apparent, the OHA decided against convening another special meeting, as done at Wingspread, and instead appointed four committees to examine those sections of the evaluation guidelines that required revision or entirely new material. After a year's work, the committees presented their proposals to the members of the Association at the annual meeting in Galveston, Texas, in 1989, where their reports were discussed, amended, and adopted at the general business meeting.

During the next year, the chairs of the four evaluation guidelines committees analyzed, revised, and expanded the Goals and Guidelines into a new Statement of Principles and Standards. They offered these standards for amendment and adoption by the membership at the annual meeting in Cambridge, Massachusetts, in November 1990.

If that process sounds convoluted, it was. But its many stages were designed deliberately to foster thoughtful debate among the widest cross-section of oral history practitioners. As a result, the new standards and guidelines more specifically addressed the needs of independent and unaffiliated researchers, as well as those of the larger oral history programs and archives. They dealt with the problems and potentials of videotaped interviews. They raised issues about the use of oral history in the classroom by teachers and students.

The most intense discussions predictably dealt with ethical issues. A greater awareness of the effects of race, class, gender, ethnicity, and culture on interviewing, together with a heightened concern over the impact that the oral history projects might have on the communities in which the interviews were conducted, were woven into both the Evaluation Guidelines and the Statement of Principles and Standards. The new guidelines and standards encouraged oral historians to make their interviews accessible to the community and to consider sharing the rewards and recognition that might result from their projects with their interviewees. They also sanctioned the use of anonymous interviews, although only in "extremely sensitive" circumstances.

During the 1990s, the rapid advances in technology required yet another revision on the new ways of recording, preserving, using and distributing oral history. In 1998 an ad hoc committee presented additional revisions for discussion and adoption by the membership at the annual meeting in Buffalo, New York. These revisions included new sections on recording equipment and tape preservation, and aimed to encourage practitioners to pay more attention to technical standards and to new technology and media, particularly the Internet. At the same time they raised some of the ethical issues that the new technology posed.

All of those who labored in the preparation of the principles and standards and the evaluation guidelines trust that they will offer positive assistance to anyone conducting oral history interviews. While these guidelines and standards provide a basis for peer judgment and review, their success will ultimately depend more on the willingness of the individual oral historians and oral history projects to apply them to their own work.

—Donald A. Ritchie

Principles and Standards of the Oral History Association

The Oral History Association promotes oral history as a method of gathering and preserving historical information through recorded interviews with participants in past events and ways of life. It encourages those who produce and use oral history to recognize certain principles, rights, technical standards, and obligations for the creation and preservation of source material that is authentic, useful, and reliable. These include obligations to the interviewee, to the profession, and to the public, as well as mutual obligations between sponsoring organizations and interviewers.

People with a range of affiliations and sponsors conduct oral history interviews for a variety of purposes: to create archival records, for individual research, for community and institutional projects, and for publications and media productions. While these principles and standards provide a general framework for guiding professional conduct, their application may vary according to the nature of specific oral history projects. Regardless of the purpose of the interviews, oral history should be conducted in the spirit of critical inquiry and social responsibility and with a recognition of the interactive and subjective nature of the enterprise.

Responsibility to Interviewees

1. Interviewees should be informed of the purposes and procedures of oral history in general and of the aims and anticipated uses of the particular projects to which they are making their contributions.
2. Interviewees should be informed of the mutual rights in the oral history process, such as editing, access restrictions, copyrights, prior use, royalties, and the expected disposition and dissemination of all forms of the record, including the potential for electronic distribution.
3. Interviewees should be informed that they will be asked to sign a legal release. Interviews should remain confidential until interviewees have given permission for their use.
4. Interviewers should guard against making promises to interviewees that the interviewers may not be able to fulfill, such as guarantees of publication and control over the use of interviews after they have been made public. In all future uses, however, good faith efforts should be made to honor the spirit of the interviewee's agreement.
5. Interviews should be conducted in accord with any prior agreements made with the interviewee, and such agreements should be documented for the record.
6. Interviewers should work to achieve a balance between the objectives of the project and the perspectives of the interviewees. They should be sensitive to the diversity of social and cultural experiences and to the implications of race, gender, class, ethnicity, age, religion, and sexual orientation. They should encourage interviewees to respond in their own style and language and to address issues that reflect their concerns. Interviewers should fully explore all appropriate areas of inquiry with the interviewee and not be satisfied with superficial responses.
7. Interviewers should guard against possible exploitation of interviewees and be sensitive to the ways in which their interviews might be used. Interviewers must respect the rights of interviewees to refuse to discuss certain subjects, to restrict access to the interview, or, under Guidelines extreme circumstances, even to choose anonymity. Interviewers should clearly explain these options to all interviewees.
8. Interviewers should use the best recording equipment within their means to accurately reproduce the interviewee's voice and, if appropriate, other sounds as well as visual images.
9. Given the rapid development of new technologies, interviewees should be informed of the wide range of potential uses of their interviews.
10. Good faith efforts should be made to ensure that the uses of recordings and transcripts comply with both the letter and spirit of the interviewee's agreement.

Responsibility to the Public and to the Profession

1. Oral historians have a responsibility to maintain the highest professional standards in the conduct of their work and to uphold the standards of the various disciplines and professions with which they are affiliated.
2. In recognition of the importance of oral history to an understanding of the past and of the cost and effort involved, interviewers and interviewees should mutually strive to record candid information of lasting value and to make that information accessible.
3. Interviewees should be selected based on the relevance of their experiences to the subject at hand.
4. Interviewers should possess interviewing skills, as well as professional competence and knowledge of the subject at hand.
5. Regardless of the specific interests of the project, interviewers should attempt to extend the inquiry beyond the specific focus of the project to create as complete a record as possible for the benefit of others.
6. Interviewers should strive to prompt informative dialogue through challenging and perceptive inquiry. They should be grounded in the background of the persons being interviewed and, when possible, should carefully research appropriate documents and secondary sources related to subjects about which the interviewees can speak.
7. Interviewers should make every effort to record their interviews using the best recording equipment within their means to reproduce accurately the interviewee's voice and, if appropriate, image. They also should collect and record other historical documentation the interviewee may possess, including still photographs, print materials, and other sound and moving image recordings, if appropriate.
8. Interviewers should provide complete documentation of their preparation and methods, including the circumstances of the interviews.
9. Interviewers and, when possible, interviewees should review and evaluate their interviews, including any summaries or transcriptions made from them.
10. With the permission of the interviewees, interviewers should arrange to deposit their interviews in an archival repository that is capable of both preserving the interviews and eventually making them available for general use. Interviewers should provide basic information about the interviews, including project goals, sponsorship, and funding. Preferably, interviewers should work with repositories before conducting the interviews to determine necessary legal Guidelines arrangements. If interviewers arrange to retain first use of the interviews, it should be only for a reasonable time before public use.
11. Interviewers should be sensitive to the communities from which they have collected oral histories, taking care not to reinforce thoughtless stereotypes nor to bring undue notoriety to them. Interviewers should take every effort to make the interviews accessible to the communities.
12. Oral history interviews should be used and cited with the same care and standards applied to other historical sources. Users have a responsibility to retain the integrity of the interviewee's voice, neither misrepresenting the interviewee's words nor taking them out of context.
13. Sources of funding or sponsorship of oral history projects should be made public in all exhibits, media presentations, or publications that result from the projects.

14. Interviewers and oral history programs should conscientiously consider how they might share with interviewees and their communities the rewards and recognition that might result from their work.

Responsibility for Sponsoring and Archival Institutions

1. Institutions sponsoring and maintaining oral history archives have a responsibility to interviewees, interviewers, the profession, and the public to maintain the highest technical, professional, and ethical standards in the creation and archival preservation of oral history interviews and related materials.
2. Subject to conditions that interviewees set, sponsoring institutions (or individual collectors) have an obligation to: prepare and preserve easily usable records; keep abreast of rapidly developing technologies for preservation and dissemination; keep accurate records of the creation and processing of each interview; and identify, index, and catalog interviews.
3. Sponsoring institutions and archives should make known through a variety of means, including electronic modes of distribution, the existence of interviews open for research.
4. Within the parameters of their missions and resources, archival institutions should collect interviews generated by independent researchers and assist interviewers with the necessary legal agreements.
5. Sponsoring institutions should train interviewers. Such training should: provide them basic instruction in how to record high fidelity interviews and, if appropriate, other sound and moving image recordings; explain the objectives of the program to them; inform them of all ethical and legal considerations governing an interview; and make clear to interviewers what their obligations are to the program and to the interviewees.
6. Interviewers and interviewees should receive appropriate acknowledgment for their work in all forms of citation or usage.
7. Archives should make good faith efforts to ensure that uses of recordings and transcripts, especially those that employ new technologies, comply with both the letter and spirit of the interviewee's agreement.

ORAL HISTORY EVALUATION GUIDELINES

Program/Project Guidelines

Purposes and Objectives

1. Are the purposes clearly set forth? How realistic are they?
2. What factors demonstrate a significant need for the project?
3. What is the research design? How clear and realistic is it?
4. Are the terms, conditions, and objectives of funding clearly made known to judge the potential effect of such funding on the scholarly integrity of the project? Is the allocation of funds adequate to allow the project goals to be accomplished?
5. How do institutional relationships affect the purposes and objectives?

Selection of Recording Equipment

1. Should the interview be recorded on sound or visual recording equipment?
2. Are the best possible recording equipment and media available within one's budget being used?
3. Are interviews recorded on a medium that meets archival preservation standards?
4. How well has the interviewer mastered use of the equipment upon which the interview will be recorded?

Selection of Interviewers and Interviewees

1. In what ways are the interviewers and interviewees appropriate (or inappropriate) to the purposes and objectives?
2. What are the significant omissions and why were they omitted?

Records and Provenance

1. What are the policies and provisions for maintaining a record of the provenance of interviews? Are they adequate? What can be done to improve them?
2. How are records, policies, and procedures made known to interviewers, interviewees, staff, and users?
3. How does the system of records enhance the usefulness of the interviews and safeguard the rights of those involved?

Availability of Materials

1. How accurate and specific is the publicizing of the interviews?
2. How is information about interviews directed to likely users? Have new media and electronic methods of distribution been considered to publicize materials and make them available?
3. How have the interviews been used?

Finding Aids

1. What is the overall design for finding aids?
2. Are the finding aids adequate and appropriate?
3. How available are the finding aids?
4. Have new technologies been used to develop the most effective finding aids?

Management, Qualifications, and Training

1. How effective is the management of the program/project?
2. What are the provisions for supervision and staff review?
3. What are the qualifications for staff positions?
4. What are the provisions for systematic and effective training?
5. What improvements could be made in the management of the program/project?

Ethical/Legal Guidelines

What procedures are followed to assure that interviewers/programs recognize and honor their responsibility to the interviewees? Specifically, what procedures are used to assure that:

1. The interviewees are made fully aware of the goals and objectives of the oral history program/project?
2. The interviewees are made fully aware of the various stages of the program/project and the nature of their participation at each stage?
3. The interviewees are given the opportunity to respond to questions as freely as possible and are not subjected to stereotyped assumptions based on race, ethnicity, gender, class, or any other social/cultural characteristic?
4. The interviewees understand their rights to refuse to discuss certain subjects, to seal portions of the interviews, or in extremely sensitive circumstances even to choose to remain anonymous?
5. The interviewees are fully informed about the potential uses of the material, including deposit of the interviews in a repository, publication in all forms of print or electronic media, including the Internet or other emerging technologies, and all forms of public programming?
6. The interviewees are provided a full and easily comprehensible explanation of their legal rights before being asked to sign a contract or deed of gift transferring rights, title, and interest in the tape(s) and transcript(s) to an administering authority or individual?
7. Care is taken so that the distribution and use of the material complies with the letter and spirit of the interviewees' agreements?
8. All prior agreements made with the interviewees are honored?
9. The interviewees are fully informed about the potential for and disposition of royalties that might accrue from the use of their interviews, including all forms of public programming?
10. The interviews and any other related materials will remain confidential until the interviewees have released their contents?

What procedures are followed to assure that interviewers/programs recognize and honor their responsibilities to the profession? Specifically, what procedures assure that:

1. The interviewer has considered the potential for public programming and research use of the interviews and has endeavored to prevent any exploitation of or harm to interviewees?
2. The interviewer is well trained to conduct the interview in a professional manner, including the use of appropriate recording equipment and media?
3. The interviewer is well grounded in the background of the subject(s) to be discussed?
4. The interview will be conducted in a spirit of critical inquiry and that efforts will be made to provide as complete a historical record as possible?
5. The interviewees are selected based on the relevance of their experience to the subject at hand and that an appropriate cross-section of interviewees is selected for any particular project?

6. The interview materials, including recordings, transcripts, relevant photographic, moving image, and sound documents as well as agreements and documentation of the interview process, will be placed in a repository after a reasonable period of time, subject to the agreements made with the interviewee and that the repository will administer their use in accordance with those agreements?

7. The methodologies of the program/project, as well as its goals and objectives, are available for the general public to evaluate?

8. The interview materials have been properly cataloged, including appropriate acknowledgment and credit to the interviewer, and that their availability for research use is made known?

What procedures are followed to assure that interviewers and programs are aware of their mutual responsibilities and obligations? Specifically, what procedures are followed to assure that:

1. Interviewers are made aware of the program goals and are fully informed of ethical and legal considerations?

2. Interviewers are fully informed of all the tasks they are expected to complete in an oral history project?

3. Interviewers are made fully aware of their obligations to the oral history program/sponsoring institution, regardless of their own personal interest in a program/project?

4. Programs/sponsoring institutions treat their interviewers equitably by providing for appropriate compensation, acknowledging all products resulting from their work, and supporting fieldwork practices consistent with professional standards whenever there is a conflict between the parties to the interview?

5. Interviewers are fully informed of their legal rights and of their responsibilities to both the interviewee and to the sponsoring institution?

What procedures are followed to assure that interviewers and programs recognize and honor their responsibilities to the community/public? Specifically, what procedures assure that:

1. The oral history materials and all works created from them will be available and accessible to the community that participated in the project?

2. Sources of extramural funding and sponsorship are clearly noted for each interview of project?

3. The interviewers and project endeavor not to impose their own values on the community being studied?

4. The tapes and transcripts will not be used unethically?

Recording Preservation Guidelines

Recognizing the significance of the recording for historical and cultural analysis and the potential uses of oral history interviews in non-print media, what procedures are followed to assure that:

1. Appropriate care and storage of the original recordings begins immediately after their creation?

2. The original recordings are duplicated and stored according to accepted archival standards [i.e., stored in closed boxes in a cool, dry, dust-free environment]

3. Original recordings are re-duplicated onto the best preservation media before significant deterioration occurs?

4. Every effort is made in duplicating tapes to preserve a faithful facsimile of the interviewee's voice?

5. All transcribing, auditing, and other uses are done from a duplicate, not the original recording?

Tape/Transcript Processing Guidelines

Information about the Participants

1. Are the names of both interviewer and interviewee clearly indicated on the tape/abstract/transcript and in catalog materials?

2. Is there adequate biographical information about both interviewer and interviewee? Where can it be found?

Interview Information

1. Are the tapes, transcripts, time indices, abstracts, and other materials presented for use identified as to the program/project of which they are a part?

2. Are the date and place of the interview indicated on the tape, transcript, time index, and abstract and in appropriate catalog material?

3. Are there interviewers' statements about the preparation for or circumstances of the interviews? Where? Are they generally available to researchers? How are the rights of the interviewees protected against improper use of such commentaries?

4. Are there records of contracts between the program and the interviewee? How detailed are they? Are they available to researchers? If so, with what safeguards for individual rights and privacy?

Interview Tape Information

1. Is the complete original tape preserved? Are there one or more duplicate copies?

2. If the original or any duplicate has been edited, rearranged, cut, or spliced in any way, is there a record of that action, including by whom, when, and for what purposes the action was taken?

3. Do the tape label and appropriate catalog materials show the recording speed, level, and length of the interview? If videotaped, do the tape label and appropriate catalog information show the format (e.g., U-Matic, VHS, 8 mm, etc.) and scanning system and clearly indicate the tracks on which the audio and time code have been recorded?

4. In the absence of transcripts, are there suitable finding aids to give users access to information on the tapes? What form do they take? Is there a record of who prepared these finding aids?

5. Are researchers permitted to listen to or view the tapes? Are there any restrictions on the use of the tapes?

Interview Transcript Information

1. Is the transcript an accurate record of the tape? Is a careful record kept of each step of processing the transcript, including who transcribed, audited, edited, retyped, and proofread the transcripts in final copy?
2. Are the nature and extent of changes in the transcript from the original tape made known to the user?
3. What finding aids have been prepared for the transcript? Are they suitable and adequate? How could they be improved?
4. Are there any restrictions on access to or use of the transcripts? Are they clearly noted?
5. Are there any photo materials or other supporting documents for the interview? Do they enhance and supplement the text?
6. If videotaped, does the transcript contain time references and annotation describing the complementary visuals on the videotape?

Interview Content Guidelines

Does the content of each interview and the cumulative content of the whole collection contribute to accomplishing the objectives of the program/project?

1. In what particulars does each interview or the whole collection succeed or fall short of the objectives of the project or program?
2. Do audio and visual tapes in the collection avoid redundancy and supplement one another in interview content and focus?

In what ways does the program/project contribute to historical understanding?

1. In what particulars does each interview or the whole collection succeed or fall short in making such a contribution?
2. To what extent does the material add fresh information, fill gaps in the existing record, and/or provide fresh insights and perspectives?
3. To what extent is the information reliable and valid? Is it eyewitness or hearsay evidence? How well and in what manner does it meet internal and external tests of corroboration, consistency, and explication of contradictions?
4. What is the relationship of the interview information to existing documentation and historiography?
5. How does the texture of the interview impart detail, richness, and flavor to the historical record?
6. What is the nature of the information contributed? Is it facts, perceptions, interpretations, judgments, or attitudes, and how does each contribute to understanding?
7. Are the scope, volume, and representativeness of the population interviewed appropriate and sufficient to the purpose? Is there enough testimony to validate the evidence without passing the point of diminishing returns? How appropriate is the quantity to the purposes of the study?
8. How do the form and structure of the interviews contribute to making the content understandable?
9. To what extent does the audio and/or video recording capture unique sound and visual information?

10. Do the visual and other sound elements complement and/or supplement the verbal information? Has the interview captured processes, objects, or other individuals in the visual and sound environment?

Interview Conduct Guidelines

Use of Other Sources

1. Is the oral history technique the best way to acquire the information? If not, what other sources exist? Has the interviewer used them and sought to preserve them if necessary?
2. Has the interviewer made an effort to consult other relevant oral histories?
3. Is the interview technique a valuable way to supplement existing sources?
4. Do videotaped interviews complement, not duplicate, existing still or moving visual images?

Interviewer Preparation

1. Is the interviewer well informed about the subjects under discussion?
2. Are the primary and secondary sources used to prepare for the interview adequate?
3. Has the interviewer mastered the use of appropriate recording equipment and the field-recording techniques that ensure a high-fidelity recording?

Interviewee Selection and Orientation

1. Does the interviewee seem appropriate to the subjects discussed?
2. Does the interviewee understand and respond to the interview purposes?
3. Has the interviewee prepared for the interview and assisted in the process?
4. If a group interview, have composition and group dynamics been considered in selecting participants?

Interviewer-Interviewee Relations

1. Do interviewer and interviewee collaborate with each other toward interview objectives?
2. Is there a balance between empathy and analytical judgment in the interview?
3. If videotaped, is the interviewer/interviewee relationship maintained despite the presence of a technical crew? Do the technical personnel understand how a videotaped oral history interview differs from a scripted production?

Technique and Adaptive Skills

1. In what ways does the interview show that the interviewer has used skills appropriate to: the interviewee's condition (health, memory, metal alertness, ability to communicate, time schedule, etc.) and the interview location and conditions (disruptions and interruptions, equipment problems, extraneous participants, background noises, etc.)?
2. What evidence is there that the interviewer has: thoroughly explored pertinent lines of thought? Followed up on significant clues? Made an effort to identify sources of information? Employed critical challenges when needed? Thoroughly explored the potential of the visual environment, if videotaped?

3. Has the program/project used recording equipment and media that are appropriate for the purposes of the work and potential non-print as well as print uses of the material? Are the recordings of the highest appropriate technical quality? How could they be improved?
4. If videotaped, are lighting, composition, camera work, and sound of the highest appropriate technical quality?
5. In the balance between content and technical quality, is the technical quality good without subordinating the interview process?

Perspective

1. Do the biases of the interviewer interfere with or influence the responses of the interviewee?
2. What information is available that may inform the users of any prior or separate relationship between the interviewer and interviewee?

Historical Contribution

1. Does the interviewer pursue the inquiry with historical integrity?
2. Do other purposes being served by the interview enrich or diminish quality?
3. What does the interview contribute to the larger context of historical knowledge and understanding?

Independent/Unaffiliated Researcher Guidelines

Creation and Use of Interviews

1. Has the independent/unaffiliated researcher followed the guidelines for obtaining interviews as suggested in the Program/Project Guideline section?
2. Have proper citation and documentation been provided in works created (books, articles, audio-visual productions, or other public presentations) to inform users of the work about the interviews used and the permanent location of the interviews?
3. Do works created include an explanation of the interview project, including editorial procedures?
4. Has the independent/unaffiliated researcher arranged to deposit the works created in an appropriate repository?

Transfer of Interviews to Archival Repository

1. Has the independent/unaffiliated researcher properly obtained the agreement of the repository before making representations about the disposition of the interviews?
2. Is the transfer consistent with agreements or understandings with interviewees? Were legal agreements obtained from interviewees?
3. Has the researcher provided the repository with adequate descriptions of the creation of the interviews and the project?
4. What is the technical quality of the recorded interviews? Are the interviews transcribed, abstracted, or indexed, and, if so, what is the quality?

Educator and Student Guidelines

Has the educator:

1. Become familiar with the "Oral History Evaluation Guidelines" and conveyed their substance to the student?
2. Ensured that each student is properly prepared before going into the community to conduct oral history interviews, including familiarization with the ethical issues surrounding oral history and the obligation to seek the informed consent of the interviewee?
3. Become familiar with the literature, recording equipment, techniques, and processes of oral history so that the best possible instruction can be presented to the student?
4. Worked with other professionals and organizations to provide the best oral history experience for the student?
5. Considered that the project may merit preservation and worked with other professionals and repositories to preserve and disseminate these collected materials?
6. Shown willingness to share expertise with other educators, associations, and organizations?

Has the student:

1. Become thoroughly familiar with the equipment, techniques, and processes of oral history interviewing and the development of research using oral history interviews?
2. Explained to the interviewee the purpose of the interview and how it will be used and obtained the interviewee's informed consent to participate?
3. Treated the interviewee with respect?
4. Signed a receipt for and returned any materials borrowed from the interviewee?
5. Obtained a signed legal release for the interview?
6. Kept her/his word about oral or written promises made to the interviewee?
7. Given proper credit (oral or written) when using oral testimony and used the material in context?

| NOTES |

CHAPTER 1

1. *Society of the Survivors of the Riga Ghetto, Inc. v. Huttenbach*, 141 Misc. 2d 921 (1988).

2. Ibid., 928.

3. Although some of the interviews conducted by Professor Huttenbach were subsequently turned over to another historian to assist him in writing a history of the Riga Ghetto, this effort unfortunately produced another contractual dispute and more litigation. Ralph Blumenthal, "Riga Ghetto Survivors Await a Book They Can Embrace," *New York Times*, July 3, 1997, sec. C, 11.

CHAPTER 2

1. Barbara Bryant, "Thurgood Marshall Collection Press Stories Stir Furor Over LC's Opening of Papers," *Library of Congress Information Bulletin* (June 13, 1993), http://www .loc.gov//lcib/93/9312/marshall.html.

2. Ibid.

3. Harold Hongju Koh, "Unveiling Justice Blackmun," in "Symposium: Justice Blackmun and Judicial Biography: A Conversation with Linda Greenhouse," special issue, *Brooklyn Law Review* 72 (Fall 2006): 19.

4. Robert Vanni, "Deed of Gift: Caressing the Hand that Feeds," in *Libraries, Museums, and Archives: Legal Issues and Ethical Challenges in the New Information Age*, ed. Thomas A. Lipinski (Lanham, MD: The Scarecrow Press, 2002), 4.

5. Ibid., 1–2.

6. *Gifts Inter Vivos, Corpus Juris Secundum* 38A (2007), sec. 5.

7. John A. Neuenschwander, "What's In Your Legal Release Agreement?" *Oral History Association Newsletter* 41 (Fall 2007): 3. Much of the information contained in this chapter is based on seventy-two legal release agreements that were sent to the author at his request by oral history programs and independent oral historians. To the author's knowledge, all of the agreements that he surveyed and analyzed are currently in use. Various clauses drawn from these agreements are either quoted directly or paraphrased in this chapter. The author is unable to identify the program or individual contributing the agreements that are referenced because of a pledge of confidentiality that was extended to all of those who were kind enough to submit release agreements for review. The author promised that no identifying information would appear in any subsequent publication.

8. John R. Allison and Robert A. Prentice, *The Legal Environment of Business*, 5th ed. (Chicago: Dryden Press, 1991), 181.

9. Oral History Association, *Evaluation Guidelines* and *Principles and Standards of the Oral History Association* (2000), http://www.oralhistory.org/network/mw/index.php/Evaluation_Guide.

10. Library of Congress, American Folklife Center: Veterans History Project, "Interviewee's Release Form," http://www.loc.gov/vets/.

11. OHA, *Principles and Standards*.

12. OHA, *Evaluation Guidelines*.

13. *U.S. Code Annotated* 17 (2005), sec. 204 (a).

14. *Effects Associates, Inc. v. Cohen*, 908 F. 2d 555, 557 (9th Cir. 1990).

15. *Radio Television Espanola S.A. v. New World Entm't LTD*, 183 F. 3d 922, 927 (9th Cir. 1999).

16. OHA, *Evaluation Guidelines*.

17. *Black's Law Dictionary*, 5th ed. (St. Paul, MN: West Publishing Co., 1979), 1423.

18. Neuenschwander, "What's In Your Legal Release Agreement?" 8.

19. Samuel Williston and Richard A. Lord, *A Treatise on the Law of Contracts*, 4th ed., vol. 11 (St. Paul, MN: West Group, 1999), sec. 32.20, 531–532.

20. *Release, American Jurisprudence*, 66 (2008), sec. 29.

21. *Croce v. Kurnit*, 565 F.Supp. 884, 892 (D.C.N.Y. 1982).

22. OHA, *Evaluation Guidelines*.

23. OHA, *Principles and Standards*.

24. U.S. Copyright Office, *Compendium II: Copyright Office Practices*, sec. 317 (1984).

25. *Code of Federal Regulations* 45 (2007), sec. 46.117.

26. Neuenschwander, "What's In Your Legal Release Agreement?" 7.

27. OHA, *Principles and Standards*.

28. Linda P. Wood, *Oral History Projects in Your Classroom* (Oral History Association, 2001), 36 and Glenn E. Whitman, *Dialogue with the Past* (Walnut Creek, CA: AltaMira, 2004), 42.

29. Linda Shopes, "Legal and Ethical Issues in Oral History," in *Handbook of Oral History*, ed. Thomas L. Charlton, Lois E. Myers, and Rebecca Sharpless (Lanham, MD: AltaMira, 2006), 140.

Chapter 3

1. John A. Neuenschwander, "Native American Oral Tradition/History as Evidence in American Federal Courts," *Journal of the International Oral History Association* 2 (June 2004): 12.

2. *Federal Rules of Evidence*, 703.

3. *Cree v. Flores*, 157 F. 3d 762, 774 (9th Cir. 1998).

4. Robert A. Izard, *Lawyers and Lawsuits: A Guide to Litigation*, (New York: Macmillan Spectrum, 1998), 105–06.

5. John A. Neuenschwander, "What's In Your Legal Release Agreement?" *Oral History Association Newsletter* 41 (Fall 2007): 7.

6. Sam H. Bowers, "Contract of Gift" (October 24, 1983), Mississippi Department of Archives and History.

7. Robert H. McLaughlin, "From The Trench and Tower: Should Social Science Research Be Privileged?" *Law and Social Inquiry* 24 (Fall 1999): 939.

8. *In re Grand Jury Proceedings*, 5 F. 3d 397, 403 (9th Cir. 1993).

9. *Smith v. Dow Chemical Co.*, 173 F.R.D. 54, 56 (W.D.N.Y. 1997).

10. *Wilkinson v. F.B.I.*, 111 F.R.D. 432 (C.D. Cal. 1986).

11. *Anker v. G. D. Searle & Co.*, 126 F.R.D. 515, 519 (M.D.N.C. 1989).

12. *Burka v. U.S. Dept. of Health and Human Services*, 87 F. 3d 508, 521 (D.C. Cir. 1996).

13. Elizabeth C. Wiggins and Judith A. McKenna, "Court-Ordered Disclosure of Academic Research: A Clash of Science and Law," *Law and Contemporary Problems* 59 (Summer 1996): 67.

14. Oral History Association, *Principles and Standards* (2000), http://www.oralhistory.org/
network/mw/index.php/Evaluation_Guide.html.

15. Ibid.

16. *U.S. Code Annotated* 42 (2003), sec. 241 (d).

17. National Institute of Health, *Certificate of Confidentiality Kiosk: Frequently Asked Questions*,
http://grants.nih.gov/grants/policy/coc/.

18. Lisa Roy-Davis, e-mail message to H-ORALHIST@H-NET.MSU.ORG (September
20, 2007).

19. *Bonnichsen v. U.S.* 217 F. Supp. 2d 1116, 1152 (D.Or. 2002).

20. *Bonnichsen v. U.S.* 357 F. 3d 962, 979 (9th Cir. 2004).

21. *Navajo Nation v. U.S. Forest Service*, 479 F.3d 1024 (9th Cir. 9 2007), rev'd 535F. 3d
717 (9th Cir. 2008).

22. *Mochizuki v. U.S.* 43 Fed. Cl. 97 (Fed. Cl. 1999).

23. Roger A. Nowadzky, "A Comparative Analysis of Public Records Statutes," *Urban Law*
28 (1996): 65.

24. *The New York Times Co. v. City of New York Fire Dept.*, 4 N.Y. 3d 477, 488 (N.Y. 2005).

25. *Kentucky Revised Statutes*, sec. 171.400 (Michies 2006).

26. *Texas Statutes and Codes*, sec. 552.121 (Vernon's 2007).

27. Frank G. Burke, Acting Archivist of the U.S., *Procedures For Initiating Cooperative Oral
History Projects* (1985).

Chapter 4

1. *Moosally v. W.W. Norton & Co. Inc.*, 358 S.C. 320 (S.C. App. 2004).

2. Bruce W. Sanford, *Libel and Privacy*, 2nd ed. (New York: Aspen, 2002), sec. 4. 2, 97.

3. Samuel Johnson, *Idler* 45, February 24, 1759.

4. William Prosser and Page Keeton, *Prosser and Keeton on the Law of Torts*, 5th ed. (St. Paul,
MN: West Pub. Co., 1984), 771.

5. *New York Times Co. v. Sullivan*, 376 U.S. 254 (1964).

6. *Restatement (Second) of Torts*, sec. 578 (1977).

7. *Hebrew Academy of San Francisco v. Regents of University of California*, 2007 WL 388722 (Cal.
App. 1 Dist. Feb. 18, 2005).

8. Plaintiffs' Second Amended Complaint, 3–4 (March 13, 2003).

9. *Gray v. St. Martin's Press, Inc.*, 221 F. 3d 243, 250 (1st Cir. 2000).

10. *Restatement (Second) of Torts* sec. 558 (1977).

11. Richard P. Mandel & Renee Hobbs, "The Right to a Reputation After Death," *Communications and the Law* 13 (March 1991): 29.

12. Jonathan Turley, "Give the Dead Their Due," *Washington Post*, September 17, 2006, B01, http://www.washingtonpost.com/wp-dpn/content/article/2006/09/15/AR2006091500999_pf.html.

13. Richard Fausset, "William Jewell, 44, Wrongly Suspected of '96' Olympic Bombing," *Los Angeles Times*, August 8, 2007, 6.

14. Andrea H. Nadel, "What Constitutes Single Publication," *American Law Reports* 4th Series 41 (supp. 2008): sec. 541.

15. *Hebrew Academy of San Francisco. v. Goldman*, 42 Cal. 4th 883 (2007).

16. Sanford, *Libel and Privacy, sec.* 4.4, 104.

17. *Smith v. Cuban American Nat. Foundation*, 731 So. 2d 702 (Fla. App. 3 Dist. 1999).

18. Ibid., 706.

19. *Sullivan*, 376 U.S. 254 (1964).

20. *Gertz v. Robert Welch, Inc.*, 418 U.S. 323 (1974).

21. Robert M. Dato, "The Effect of Passage of Time on the Status of Inactive Public Figures," *Federal Communications and Law Journal* 35 (Fall 1983): 236.

22. *Khawar v. Globe International Inc.*, 965 P. 2d 696 (Cal. 1998).

23. *Gertz*, 418 U.S., 345.

24. *Khawar*, 704.

25. *WFAA-TV, Inc. v. McLemore*, 978 S.W. 2d 568 (Tex. 1998).

26. Ibid., 573.

27. Lloyd J. Jassin and Steven C. Schecter, *The Copyright Permission and Libel Handbook* (New York: Wiley, 1998), 111.

28. Ibid., 112–13.

29. *Street v. National Broadcasting Co.*, 645 F.2d 1227 (6th Cir. 1981).

30. Ibid., 1235.

31. Ibid., 1236.

32. *Milsap v. Journal/Sentinel Inc.*, 100 F. 3d 1265, 1269 (7th Cir. 1996).

33. Rodney A. Smolla, *Law of Defamation*, 2nd ed. (St. Paul, MN: Thomson/West, 2008), sec. 2.45, 2–65.

34. *Restatement (Second) of Torts*, sec. 578 (1977).

35. *Milkovich v. Lorain Journal Co.*, 497 U.S. 1 (1990).

36. *Levin v. McPhee*, 119 F. 3d 189 (2d Cir. 1997).

37. Ibid., 197.

38. Sanford, *Libel and Privacy*, sec. 4.12, 129–130.

39. *Partington v. Bugliosi*, 56 F. 3d 1147 (9th Cir. 1995).

40. Ibid., 1153.

41. *Katz v. Gladstone*, 673 F. Supp. 76 (D. Conn. 1987).

42. Ibid., 78.

43. Jassin, *Copyright Permission*, 118.

44. Linda Shopes, "Legal and Ethical Issues in Oral History," in *Handbook of Oral History*, ed. Thomas L. Charlton, Lois E. Myers, and Rebecca Sharpless (Lanham, MD: AltaMira, 2006), 140.

Chapter 5

1. David L. Hudson Jr., *Privacy and Newsgathering*, First Amendment Center, http://www.firstamendmentcenter.org.

2. *Restatement (Second) of Torts* sec. 652E (1977).

3. John L. Diamond, Lawrence C. Levine, and M. Stuart Madden, *Understanding Torts*, 3rd ed. (Newark, NJ: LexisNexis MathewBender, 2007), 391.

4. Mathew Stohl, "False Light Invasion of Privacy in Docudramas: The Oxymoron Which Must Be Solved," *Akron Law Review* 35 (2002), fn9.

5. J. Thomas McCarthy, *Rights of Publicity and Privacy*, 2nd ed., vol. 1 (St. Paul, MN: Thomson/West, 2003), sec. 1:22, 1–31-32.

6. "State Law: False Light," Citizens Media Law Project, http://www.citimedialaw.org/legal-guide/state-law-false-light (last visited 3/4/09).

7. Rodney A. Smolla, *Law of Defamation*, 2nd ed. (St. Paul, MN: Thomson/West, 2007), sec. 10:13, 10–17 &18.

8. *Cantrell v. Forest City Pub. Co.*, 419 U.S. 245, 247 (1974).

9. Ibid.

10. *Raveling v. HarperCollins Publishers Inc.*, F. 3d, 2005 WL 900232 (C.A.7 (Ill), Mar. 4, 2005).

11. Smolla, *Law of Defamation*, sec. 10:19-21, 10-22.2-4.

12. *Seale v. Gramercy Pictures*, 964 F. Supp. 918, 928 (E.D. Pa. 1997).

13. *Restatement (Second) of Torts* sec. 652D (1977).

14. Diamond, *Understanding Torts*, 392.

15. *Haynes v. Alfred A. Knopf, Inc,.* 8 F. 3d 1222 (7th Cir. 1993).

16. Ibid., 1224-25.

17. Ibid., 1230.

18. *Uranga v. Federated Publications, Inc.*, 138 Idaho 550, 557, (2003).

19. *Perry v. Columbia Broadcasting System Inc.*, 499 F. 2d 797 (7th Cir. 1974).

20. Ibid., 799.

21. Ibid.

22. Ibid., 800.

23. David A. Elder, *Privacy Torts* (St. Paul, MN: Thomson/West, 2002), sec. 3:18, 3–196.

24. Valerie Raleigh Yow, *Recording Oral History*, 2nd ed. (Walnut Creek, CA: AltaMira, 2005), 127.

25. *Showler v. Harper's Magazine Foundation*, 222 Fed. Appx. 755, 2007 WL 867188 (C.A. 10 (Okla.) Mar. 3, 2007).

26. *Restatement (Second) of Torts* sec. 652C (1977).

27. John A. Neuenschwander, "What's In Your Legal Release Agreement?" *Oral History Association Newsletter* 41 (Fall 2007): 3.

28. *Tellado v. Time-Life Books, Inc.*, 643 F. Supp. 904 (D.N.J.1986).

29. Ibid., 905–06.

30. Ibid., 906.

31. *Lane v. Random House, Inc.*, 985 F. Supp. 141 (D. D.C. 1995).

32. Lloyd J. Jassin and Steven C. Schecter, *The Copyright Permissions and Libel Handbook* (New York: Wiley, 1998), 151.

CHAPTER 6

1. Saunders & Silverstein LLP, *Legal Fixation Blog,* "Four Most Mythical Copyright Myths," July 18, 2007, http://massiplaw.com/massiplas/ (last visited 10/07/08).

2. U.S. Const., art. 1, sec. 8.

3. *U.S. Code Annotated* 17 (2005), sec. 102.

4. Ibid, Sec. 101.

5. Marshall Leaffer, *Understanding Copyright Law,* 4th ed. (Newark, NJ: LexisNexis, 2005), 93.

6. William F. Patry, *Patry on Copyright,* vol. 2 (St. Paul, MN: Thomson Reuters/West, 2008), sec. 3:63, 3–176.

7. *Feist Publications, Inc. v. Rural Telephone Services Co. Inc.,* 499 U.S. 340 (1991).

8. *Maxtone-Graham v. Burtchaell,* 803 F.2d 1253 (2d Cir. 1986).

9. *Nash v. CBS Inc.,* 899 F.2d 1537, 1541 (7th Cir. 1990).

10. *U.S. Code Annotated* 17 (2005), sec. 102.

11. Ibid., sec. 204 (a).

12. *Radio Television Espanola S.A., v. New World Entm't LTD,* 183 F. 3d 922, 927 (9th Cir. 1999).

13. *U.S. Code Annotated* 17 (2005), sec. 101.

14. Paul Goldstein, *Copyright,* 3rd ed. (New York: Aspen Publishers, Inc., 2007), sec. 4.2.1.3, 4–19 & 21.

15. Patry, *Patry on Copyright,* vol. 2, sec. 5:19, 5–63.

16. *Berman v. Johnson,* 518, F. Supp. 2d 791 (E. D. Va. 2007).

17. *Rubin v. Boston Magazine Co.,* 645 F. 2d 80 (1st Cir. 1981).

18. U.S. Copyright Office, *Compendium II, Copyright Office Practices,* sec. 317 (1984).

19. Robert A Gorman, *Copyright Law,* 2nd ed. (Washington, DC: Federal Judicial Center, 2006), 70.

20. Leaffer, *Understanding Copyright,* 203–04.

21. *U.S. Code Annotated* 17 (2005), sec. 201 (a).

22. Ibid., sec. 101 (1).

23. Ibid., sec.101 (2).

24. CCNV *v. Reid*, 490 U.S. 730 (1989).

25. Gorman, *Copyright Law*, 74.

26. *Aymes v. Bonnelli*, 980 F.2d 857, 864 (2nd Cir. 1992).

27. Gorman, *Copyright Law*, 74.

28. *U.S. Code* Annotated 17 (2005), sec. 101.

29. Stephen Fishman, *The Copyright Handbook: What Every Writer Needs to Know*, 10th ed. (Berkeley, CA: Nolo, 2008), 216.

30. U.S. Copyright Office, *Termination of Transfers and Licenses Under 17 U.S.C. sec. 203*, http://www.copyright.gov/docs/203.html.

31. Fishman, *The Copyright Handbook*, 214.

32. *U.S. Code Annotated* 17 (2005), sec. 106 (1–5).

33. Tom Kindre, *The Boys of New Jersey* (Victoria, BC: Trafford Publishing Co., 2004), Author's Note.

34. Fishman, *The Copyright Handbook*, 281.

35. U.S. Copyright Office, *Copyright Basics*, www.copyright.gov.

36. *U.S. Code Annotated* 17(2005), sec. 107(1–4).

37. Mary Minow, *How I Learned to Love FAIR USE*, Stanford Fair Use Center, http://fairuse.stanford.edu/.

38. *Harper & Row Publishers, Inc. v. Nation Enterprises*, 471 U.S. 539 (1985).

39. *Payne v. The Courier-Journal*, F. Supp. 2d 2005. WL 1287434, (W.D. Ky., May 31, 2005).

40. *Payne v. The Courier-Journal*, 193 Fed Appx. 397, 2006 WL 2075345 (C.A. 6 Ky., July 25, 2006).

41. *Love v. Kwitny*, 706 F. Supp. 1123, 1134 (S.D.N.Y. 1989).

42. *Love v. Kwitny*, 772 F. Supp. 1367 (S.D.N.Y. 1991).

43. *Jacobsen v. Deseret Book Co.*, 287 F. 3d 936, 946 (10th Cir. 2002).

44. *Jacobsen v. Deseret Book Co.*, F. Supp. 2d, WL 1806858 (D. Utah, Jan. 12, 2001), rev'd 287 F. 3d 936 (10th Cir. 2002).

45. Ibid.

46. Leaffer, *Understanding Copyright*, 506.

47. Fishman, *The Copyright Handbook*, 329–30.

48. Ibid., 53.

49. Jerry Brito and Bridget Dooling, "An Orphan Works Affirmative Defense to Copyright Infringement Actions," *Michigan Telecommunications Technology Law Review* 12 (2005): 76.

50. U.S. Copyright Office, *Report on Orphan Works: A Report of the Register of Copyrights*, (2006), 1, www.copyright.gov/.

51. Letter to Jule L. Sigall, U.S. Copyright Office from Arnita A. Jones, Executive Director, Amer. Hist. Assoc., March 25, 2005, www.copyright.gov/.

52. Fishman, *The Copyright Handbook*, 429.

53. Idaho State Historical Society, "DNI Inventory," http://www.idahohistory.net/dni, (last visited 11/30/07).

54. University of Illinois at Springfield, *Guide to the Oral History Collection*, http://www.uis .edu/archives/contents/htm, (last visited 1/22/08).

55. District of Columbia Public Library, *Oral History Collection*, http://dcpl.dc.gov/dcpl/ cwp/view.asp?a+12648&q+566723, (last visited 10/17/08).

56. Fishman, *The Copyright Handbook*, 144.

57. *U.S. Code Annotated* 17 (2005), sec. 101.

58. Donald A. Ritchie, *Doing Oral History*, 2nd ed. (New York: Oxford University Press, 2003), 182.

59. Donald A. Ritchie, e-mail message to author (October 27, 2008).

60. Ellen M. Kozak, *Every Writer's Guide to Copyright and Publishing Law*, 3rd ed. (New York: Henry Holt, 2004), 94.

Chapter 7

1. Civil Rights in Mississippi Digital Archives, The McCain Library & Archives, University of Southern Mississippi, "Intellectual Property and Privacy Information," http://www.lib.usm/=spcol/crda/index. html, (last visited 1/6/08).

2. Ibid.

3. Copyright & Fair Use Center, "Website Permissions," Stanford University Libraries, http:/fairuse.standford.edu/Copyright_and_Fair_Use_Overview/Chapter6/6–6html, (last visited 10/28/08).

4. Stephen Fishman, *The Copyright Handbook: What Every Writer Needs to Know*, 10th ed. (Berkeley, CA: Nolo, 2008), 164.

5. Ibid., 343.

6. *Los Angeles Times v. Free Republic*, F. Supp 2nd, 2000 WL 1863566 (C.D. Cal. Nov. 16, 2000).

7. *Intellectual Reserve, Inc. v. Utah Lighthouse Ministry, Inc.*, 75 F. Supp. 2d 1290 (D. Utah, 1999).

8. University of Alaska Fairbanks' Project Jukebox, "Use of Jukebox Programs," http://uaf-db.uaf.edu/Jukebox/PJWeb/progusecha.htm (last visited 1/6/08).

9. *Matteo v. Rubin*, F. Supp. 2d, 2007 WL 4294734 (N.D. Ill., Dec. 3, 2007).

10. *Firth v. State*, 98 N.Y. 2d 365, 371–72 (2002).

11. LegalMatch, *Click Wrap License Lawyers*, http://www.legalmatch.com/law-library/article/click-wrap-license.html (last visited 10/30/08).

12. *Marobie-FL, Inc. v. National Ass'n of Fire Equipment Distributors*, 983 F. Supp. 1167 (N.D. Ill. 1997).

13. Densho Digital Archives, The Japanese American Legacy Project "Agreement & Application," http://www.densho.org/archive/register.asp (last visited 10/1/07).

14. University of Alaska Fairbanks, "Use of Jukebox Programs."

15. Regional Oral History Office, The Bancroft Library, UC Berkeley Library, "Oral History Online," http://bancroft.berkeley.edu/ROHO/collections/ohonline.html (last visited 1/22/08).

16. The Rutgers Oral History Archives, http://oralhistory.rutgers.edu/Interviews/lauffer_robert.html (last visited 1/22/08).

17. The New South Voices, University of No. Carolina at Charlotte, "Copyright," http://newsouthvoices.uncc.edu/about/contact.php (last visited 1/3/08).

18. Maria Rogers Oral History Program of The Carnegie Branch Library for Local History, "Oral History Digital Archive," http://www.bplcarnegie.org/oralHistory/overview.cfm (last visited 1/2/08).

19. Bland County History Archives, http://www. bland.k12.va.us/bland/rocky/gap.html (last visited 12/26/07).

20. Bridgeport Public Library, "Bridgeport Working: Voices from the 20th Century," http://www.bridgeporthistory.org/intro.cfm (last visited 1/3/08).

21. Shenandoah Valley Oral History Project, http://publichistory.jmu.edu/SVOHP/ (last visited 1/29/08).

22. *U.S. Code Annotated* 17 (2007), sec. 107.

23. Oral History Association, *Principles and Standards* (2000), http://www.oralhistory.org/network/mw/index.php/Evaluation_Guide.

CHAPTER 8

1. "IRBs and Behavioral and Social Science Research: Finding the Middle Ground," *AAHRPP Advance*, http://www.aahrpp.org/Documents/D000165.PDF (October 24, 2008).

2. Patricia Cohen, "As Ethics Panels Expand Grip, No Field Is Off Limits," *New York Times*, Feb. 28, 2007, sec. A, 15.

3. Philip Hamburger, "The New Censorship: Institutional Review Boards," *Supreme Court Review* (2004): 273–75.

4. *Application of the Department of Health and Human Services Regulations for the Protection of Human Subjects at 45 CFR Part 46, Subpart A to Oral History Interviewing*, OHRP (2003) at http://www.hhs.gov/ohrp/policy/index.html.

5. Donald A. Ritchie, *Doing Oral History*, 2nd ed. (New York: Oxford University Press, 2003), 219.

6. Linda Shopes, "Negotiating Institutional Review Boards," *Perspectives: The Newsmagazine of the American Historical Association* 45, no. 3 (Mar. 2007): 39.

7. Oral History Association, *Principles and Standards* (2000), http://www.oralhistory.org/network/mw/index.php/Evaluation_Guide.

8. Robert B. Townshend, "The Feds and IRBs: Your Opportunity to Weigh in," *AHA Today*, (November 6, 2007), http://blog.historians.org/profession/372/the-feds-and-irbs-your-opportunity-to-weigh-in.

9. OHRP *Policy Statement on Oral History*.

10. Ibid.

11. E. Taylor Atkins, "Oral History and IRBs: An Update from the 2006 HRPP Conference," *Perspectives: The Newsletter of the American Historical Association* 45, no. 3 (March 2007), 42.

12. American Association of University Professors, *Academic Freedom and the Institutional Review Board* (2006), http://www.aaup.ort/AAUPcomm/re[/A/humansubs.html.

13. Bruce Bridgeman, "AAUP Misperceives IRB Challenges," *Academe Online* (January-February 2007), http://www.aaup.org/AAUP/purres/academe/2007/JF/LTE/IRB.htm.

14. Ibid.

15. Ibid.

16. University of Michigan, Human Research Protection Program, "Determining Whether Research Involves Human Subjects, B. Illustrations," *Operations Manual* (Nov. 2007), http://www.research.umich.edu /hrpp/om/Part4.pdf (last visited 1/09/08).

17. Mona Moore, Assistant Admistration Manager, University of Michigan Human Research Protection Program, e-mail message to the author (January 24, 2008).

18. University of Texas, Office of Research Support and Compliance, "Oral History Policy Update," (May 18, 2004), http://www.utexas.edu/research/rsc/humanresearch/special_topics/policy_updates.php (last visited 1/07/08).

19. Columbia University Institutional Review Board, "IRB Review of Oral History Projects," http://www.columbia.edu/cu/irb/policies/documents/OralHistoryPolicy Final.012308 .pdf (last visited 10/30/08).

20. Ibid.

21. Mary Marshal Clark, Director, OHRO, e-mail message to author (October 25, 2008).

22. Ibid.

23. Ibid.

24. Cohen, "As Ethics Panels Expand Grip," *New York Times*.

25. Ritchie, *Doing Oral History*, 220.

Chapter 9

1. Valerie Yow, e-mail message to the author (February 3, 2005).

2. Jennifer Bagby, "Note, Justifications For State Bystander Intervention Statutes," *Indiana Law Review* 33 (2000): 572.

3. *Ed Rachal Foundation v. D'Unger*, 207 S.W. 3d 330, 333 (Tex. 2006).

4. *U.S. Code Annotated* 18 (2005), sec. 4.

5. *Crime of omission-Misprision of felony, American Jurisprudence Criminal Law* 21(2008), sec. 32.

6. *In re Calonge*, 52 A.D. 3d 1111 (N.Y. 2008).

7. Wayne R. LaFave, *Substantive Criminal Law*, 2nd ed. (Eagan, MN: Thomson/West, 2003), sec. 13.6(b), 409–410.

8. *State v. Carson*, 274 S.C. 316, 317 (S.C. 1980).

9. *South Carolina Attorney General Opinion* 90–28, 1990 S.C. WL 482416.

10. Ibid.

11. Ibid.

12. *South Dakota Codified Laws*, Title 22–11–12 (Supp. 2008).

13. *Ohio Revised Code Annotated* sec. 2921.22(A) (Page's Supp. 2008).

14. Gabriel D. M. Ciociola, "Misprision of Felony and Its Progeny," *Brandeis Law Journal* 41 (Summer 2003): 728.

15. *Wisconsin Statutes* sec. 939.74 (2005–06).

16. Oral History Association, *Principles and Standards* (2000), http://www.oralhistory.org/network/mw/index.php/Evaluation_Guide.

17. Ibid.

18. American Sociological Association, *Code of Ethics* sec. 11.01 (b) (1999) http://www.asanet.org.

19. Ibid., sec. 11.02 (a).

20. Ibid.

21. Valerie Yow, *Recording Oral History*, 2nd ed. (Walnut Creek, CA: AltaMira, 2005), 129.

22. *Roberts v. U. S.*, 445 U.S. 552, 558 (1980).

| SUGGESTIONS FOR
FURTHER READING |

COPYRIGHT

Fishman, Stephen. *The Copyright Handbook: What Every Writer Needs to Know*. 10th ed. Berkeley, CA: Nolo, 2008.

Kozak, Ellen M. *Every Writer's Guide to Copyright and Publishing Law*. 3rd ed. New York: Henry Holt, 2004.

Leaffer, Marshall. *Understanding Copyright Law*. 4th ed. Newark, NJ: LexisNexis, 2005.

DEFAMATION AND PRIVACY

Diamond, John L., Lawrence C. Levine, and M. Stuart Madden. *Understanding Torts*. 3rd ed. Newark, NJ: LexisNexis MathewBender, 2007.

Jassin, Lloyd J., and Steven C. Schecter. *The Copyright Permission and Libel Handbook*. New York: Wiley, 1998.

Sanford, Bruce W. *Libel and Privacy*. 2nd ed. New York: Aspen, 2002.

ORAL HISTORY

Charlton, Thomas L., Lois E. Myers, and Rebecca Sharpless, eds. *Handbook of Oral History*. Lanham, MD: AltaMira, 2006.

Perks, Robert and Alistair Thomson, eds. *The Oral History Reader*. 2nd ed. New York: Routledge, 2006.

Ritchie, Donald A. *Doing Oral History*. 2nd ed. New York: Oxford University Press, 2003.

Trimble, Charles, Barbara Sommer, and Mary Kay Quinlan. *The American Indian Oral History Manual*. Walnut Creek, CA: Left Coast Press, 2008.

Yow, Valerie Raleigh. *Recording Oral History*: A Guide for the Humanities and Social Sciences. 2nd ed. Walnut Creek, CA: AltaMira, 2005.

| RECOMMENDED WEB SITES |

Copyright & Fair Use Center, Stanford University Libraries
http://fairuse.stanford.edu/
Articles, news, featured cases, blogs, and links to other useful Web sites.
Creative Commons
http://creativecommons.org/
A not-for-profit organization that encourages copyright holders to take a less restrictive view than copyright holders traditionally have of how their works may be utilized by others. They provide tools such as Creative Commons licenses that allow copyright holders to reserve certain rights but waive others for the benefit of future creators.
First Amendment Center
http://firstamendmentcenter.org/
Comprehensive research coverage of key First Amendment issues and topics, daily news, a library, links to other Web Sites, and analysis by respected legal specialists.
Institutional Review Blog
http://www.Institutional review blog.com/2008/07/political-science-perspectives-on-irbs.html
News and commentary about IRBs' oversight of humanities and social science research.
Oral History Association
http://www.oralhistory.org/

Information on resources for historians, librarians and archivists, students, journalists, and teachers, including OHA publications and conferences. Provides links to the H-OralHist listserv, OHA Network, OHA Wiki, and *Oral History Review.*

United States Copyright Office

www.copyright.gov

Information on filing for copyright registration, enforcement, and laws, including more than seventy-five circulars and factsheets on key copyright issues such as *Copyright Basics, Works Made for Hire Under 1976 Copyright Act,* and *Copyright Registration for Online Works.*

| INDEX |

THE OXFORD ORAL HISTORY SERIES

J. Todd Moye (University of North Texas), Kathryn Nasstrom (University of San Francisco),
and Robert Perks (The British Library Sound Archive), *Series Editors*
Donald A. Ritchie, *Senior Advisor*

Doing Oral History, Second Edition
Donald A. Ritchie

Approaching an Auschwitz Survivor: Holocaust Testimony and its Transformations
Edited by Jürgen Matthäus

A Guide to Oral History and the Law
John A. Neuenschwander

CPSIA information can be obtained at www.ICGtesting.com
Printed in the USA
BVOW011530300912

301730BV00002B/22/P

9 780195 365962